Only in FLORIDA

WHY DID THE MANATEE CROSS THE ROAD
& Other True Tales

CAREN SCHNUR NEILE

THE
History
PRESS

Published by The History Press
Charleston, SC
www.historypress.com

Copyright © 2020 by Caren Schnur Neile
All rights reserved

Landscape cover images courtesy of Steve Morrison.

First published 2020

Manufactured in the United States

ISBN 9781467143066

Library of Congress Control Number: 2019954266

Notice: The information in this book is true and complete to the best of our knowledge. It is offered without guarantee on the part of the author or The History Press. The author and The History Press disclaim all liability in connection with the use of this book.

All rights reserved. No part of this book may be reproduced or transmitted in any form whatsoever without prior written permission from the publisher except in the case of brief quotations embodied in critical articles and reviews.

For my students and teachers—past, present and future

And for Miles Abraham, who has a standing invitation here

CONTENTS

Acknowledgments 7
Introduction: Florida Folks 9

PART 1. "I'm Really Proud of You, Dad": People and Places
1. Harry Potter and the Loving Father 23
2. I Would Only Let Burt Reynolds Do That 27
3. The Other Side of Paradise 32
4. A Jewish Boy in Jacksonville 37
5. Elevator to the Shallows 41
6. Integrating the University of Florida 46
7. Fakahatchee Archaeology 50
8. A Mar-a-Lago Memory 54
9. Help Wanted: Must Farm 59
10. A Bibliothèque in Miami Gardens 63
11. How Much Is Enough? 67
12. Golf, Of Course 71
13. Teaching the Holocaust 75

PART 2. "It's a Copper Whopper!": Water and Weather
14. The FlatsMaster 81
15. The Costume Must Go On 86
16. How One New Yorker Came to Love Florida 90
17. Why Did the Manatee Cross the Road? 94

CONTENTS

18. There's No Place Like Home	98
19. Ballast	103
20. The Sponger and the Seabird	110
21. Surfing with Dolphins	114
22. When Lightning Strikes	118
23. Muck in My Moccasins	123

PART 3. "A *GALLO* IN MIAMI?": FAUNA AND FLORA

24. The Last *Gringo* in Hialeah	129
25. Aunt Minnie Mae Gets Supper	133
26. Pelican Urgent Care	137
27. In Dog We Trust	141
28. The Kite Whisperer	145
29. Her First Crab	150
30. Hanging with the Gators	154
31. A Turtle Love Story	159
32. Beating the Blues	164
33. The Nature of Nature	169
Selected Bibliography	173
About the Author	175

ACKNOWLEDGMENTS

Thank you, Joe Gartrell, for believing both in this project and in me. Thanks also to Michelle Andrews, Samantha Harris, Anesti Karastinos, Bilha Ron and Joe Thomas for helping me connect with some of the people and stories that made this book what it is.

Thank you, Tom Neile, for always supporting me, no matter what, when, how, where or why.

Most importantly, my sincere appreciation goes out to the people who contributed so generously of their time, patience and stories to make this book possible.

Anthony Armonda
Beckyjo Bean
Grace Briden
Patricia Burdett
Arthur Cohen
Eva Cohen
Joseph DeCelles
Carl Fields
Sol Friedman
Lucia Gonzalez
Shirlee [Hammond]
Steve [Hammond]
Becky Harris
Diamond-Storm Hosch
Anastasios Karastinos
Holly Larson, PhD
Lucrèce Louisdhon-Louinis
Laurie Martin
Steve Morrison
Pat Nease
Kitty Oliver, PhD
Janixx Parisi
Eddie Rennolds
Samuel Ron
Ramona Rung
Alexander Suarez
Bill Trapani, PhD
Mark Traugott
Joel Vinikoor, DPM
Lori Vinikoor, DPM
Sheldon Voss
Peter Wegmann
Rodney Welch
Tanya Wilson
Pedro Zepeda

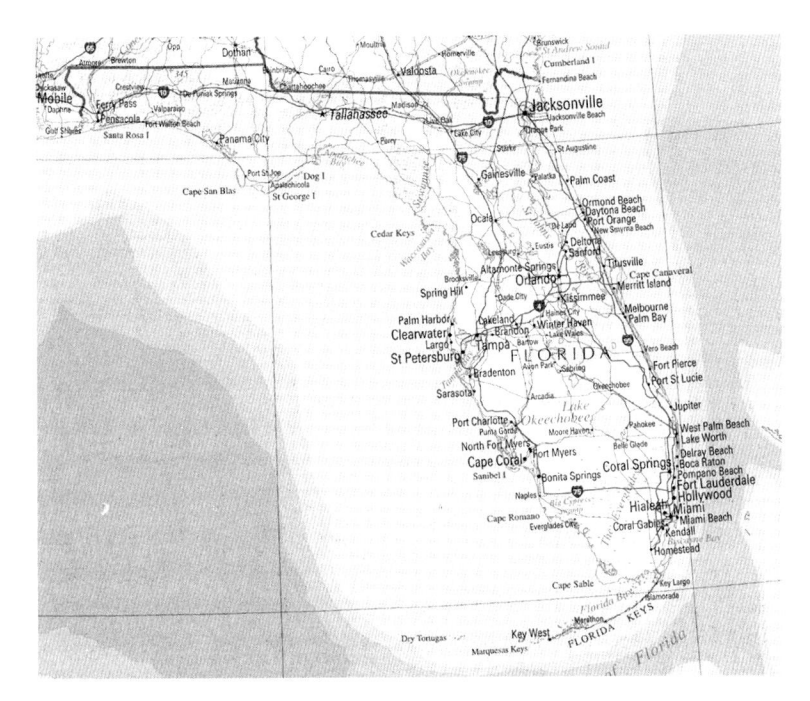

A map of Florida. *University of Texas/yellowmaps.com*.

INTRODUCTION

FLORIDA FOLKS

*Sometimes I think I've figured out some order in the universe,
but then I find myself in Florida, swamped by incongruity and paradox,
and I have to start all over again.*
—Susan Orlean

I love Florida, and I venture to say that I love it like only a nonnative can. Don't they say converts make the truest believers? I suggest that only someone who grew up far away from this troubled paradise is able to fully appreciate the things natives can take for granted: the diversity of culture and lifestyles, the (more or less) balmy weather, the amazing cast of characters current and historical, the flora and fauna, the truly unique wetlands—and did I mention the weather?

Since the Spanish landed in 1513, and for thousands of years before that, people have enjoyed the magnificent expanse of Florida land and sky that always puts me in mind of a snow globe—mainly flat on the bottom, with 180 degrees of arcing heavens above. And as memorable as the beaches, the Everglades, the cattle country and all the rest are the people. It's safe to say that we've had more than our share of pirates and profiteers, drug dealers and dirt bags, but we've also got more than sixty-five thousand square miles of some of the hardest working, most generous, fascinating people you'd ever want to meet. (Over twenty-one million of them, in fact.)

Of course, you could say that sort of thing about a lot of places. Meanwhile, most of us are pretty ordinary. So just what makes ordinary Floridians interesting? Maybe it's the mix of people and place.

Introduction

FLORIDA MAN (AND WOMAN)

It's always sunny in the Sunshine State. Except at night.
—Jarod Kintz

Just when you thought it was safe to go to Florida, a December 20, 2018 headline in the *Miami Herald* appeared that read "Florida Man 2018, A Look Back at Florida's Most Florida Crime Stories." If you think that headline has a typo, you're not alone. But what it means is that to outsiders, these stories have the strongest Floridian flavor. That is, they are the strangest. Included in the mix: A Florida man told the Dania Beach police that he was carrying his "daily vitamins." The pills turned out to be heroin. Or try this: A Florida man exited a men's room at Daytona Beach International Airport wearing only black socks. (You guessed it, another drug-related story.) A Florida woman (we are equal opportunists here) in St. Petersburg called 911 to ask for a beer delivery. And perhaps my favorite: A Florida man walked into a Brookville department store for a job interview and came out with two stolen pairs of shoes.

The blurb beneath the headline reads: "We don't know what it is about Florida. Or Florida Man and Florida Woman. Maybe it's the heat. Maybe it's the humidity. Maybe it's the red tide. Because people sure tend to behave differently down here than other parts of the nation."

So what is this Florida Man? I had never heard of him myself until about a year ago. According to knowyourmeme.com, the Florida Man meme has spawned a beer, a documentary, fan art and non-Florida derivatives such as Colombian Man and Shirtless Man. Here is the explanation, lightly edited:

> *Florida Man is a Twitter feed that curates news headline descriptions of bizarre domestic incidents involving a male subject residing in the state of Florida The tweets are meant to be humorously read as if they were perpetrated by a single individual dubbed "the world's worst superhero."*

The @FloridaMan Twitter feed, which was launched on January 26, 2013, features news headlines containing the keywords "Florida man." Within one month, the account garnered over sixty-four thousand followers. What's more, according to *Washington Post Magazine*, a "Florida Man Challenge" went viral in March 2019. Millions did an Internet search for their birthdays and the term "Florida Man" and found legitimate news headlines for every day of the year. Headlines such as: "Florida Man Steals $300 Worth of Sex

Introduction

Toys While Dressed as Ninja"; "Florida Man Drinks Goat Blood in Ritual Sacrifice, Runs for Senate." You get the picture?

As you can see, bizarre behavior abounds. I would hazard a guess that the temperature doesn't have as much to do with Florida Man as do the long hours of subtropical sunlight (experts note that crime seems to experience an uptick in the summer months), the live-and-let-live lifestyle, the diversity of people and cultures and the *sheer size* of this great state. In other words, it's not the heat. It's the humanity.

Try not to groan; I have chosen not to include the most bizarre stories here, for the simple reason that the Florida men and women I met across the state were simply not bizarre. They were, in fact, as normal as you or me. (At least they were as normal as me!) Unbelievable Florida Man stories? Those could fill a dozen books, but I don't know how many people would relate to them or get a good idea of what Floridians are really like. Consider this, then, a mild (but still entertaining!) antidote to those crazy Florida Man stories.

A DOZEN FUN FACTS ABOUT FLORIDA

People throw shade at Florida. Like, a lot. But you can't put shade on us. We're the Sunshine State!
—Lane Pittman

To put what you are going to read into some sort of context, here are a few things that are helpful to know about Florida.

1. It ranks third by population in the country, after California and Texas.
2. It is the eighth-most densely populated state in the union.
3. About 6.5 percent of American residents live in Florida.
4. Its southernmost tip, Key West, is just ninety miles from Cuba.
5. It is the only state that contains a region with a subtropical climate.
6. It is one of only seven states with no personal income tax.
7. The archipelago known as the Florida Keys comprises 1,700 islands.
8. St. Augustine was the first area settled by Europeans in North America.
9. Orlando attractions bring in more tourists than any other amusement park destination in the country.
10. Key West's average temperature is the highest in the United States.

Introduction

11. About 65 percent of residents were not born here, resulting in the largest nonnative percentage of a state population behind Nevada.
12. In the United States, Florida has been designated "ground zero" for the debilitating effects of climate change, with South Florida slated for the worst, earliest effects.

PUBLIC STORYTELLING

Two things Florida can teach the other 49 states: how to make a good margarita and how to deal with the aftermath of a hurricane.
—Tom Feeney

The idea for this book grew out of a segment I've coproduced and cohosted with local legend Michael Stock for over a decade on South Florida public radio WLRN called the Public Storyteller. As a performance storyteller and university professor of storytelling studies, one of my greatest pleasures is to help others tell their stories, to give voice to the widest possible range of people and experience. I truly believe it's a form of social activism and public service. Why, you ask? Because it's a truism among storytellers: "You can't hate somebody once you know their story." It's the first and most important step to true understanding, because you are taking a walk in their shoes, experiencing their world through their eyes.

So the segment, on Michael Stock's amazing, and amazingly long-running, show *Folk & Acoustic Music*, features locals telling brief stories that happened to them in the region—in their own words, without performance tricks or fluff. The idea is that if you hear a mother tell about her son's experience at a Metrorail station in Miami and you've never met her nor heard of the Metrorail, you've become connected in the seven minutes it's taken her to tell her story with both a person and a place in your community. Then if you read a news story about the Metrorail, or you have to vote on light rail, you have a frame of reference. It's that simple.

After each story airs, Michael and I discuss it: he from the perspective of a listener, and I from the perspective of a storyteller. Since the segment's inception in 2007, we've featured hundreds of people, one every Sunday afternoon at 4:00 p.m.

Anyway, partly because the concept for this book grew from that segment, I chose to include stories that I've heard rather than read. In each case, I personally met the storyteller, at least by telephone, but more often in person. In-person storytelling is best, of course, because then you get the nuances of the story through body language, including facial expressions. But I venture to say that any oral storytelling is going to give you a more authentic version of a personal story than if the subject had written it down. It's more pure, less adulterated and polished. More about that later.

WHY THIS BOOK

I live in Florida and people are crazy here. And I say that lovingly.
—Amy Seimetz

In 1983, a friend and I planned a trip from New York City to Alaska. I got my driver's license just for the occasion, and we bought a used car. We also bought camping gear. We thought we were prepared. And then my uncle gave me a going-away present: journalist Joe McGinniss's Alaskan masterpiece (in my opinion, at least) *Going to Extremes*. The book tells the stories of diverse people all over Alaska and how they were affected by the 1970s oil boom.

Now, I am not suggesting that this book should remind you of that one. For one thing, the chapters about each person are far longer and more in-depth than those here. For another, McGinniss is a genius. But after reading *Going to Extremes*, I felt like I had a handle on Alaska, because I had a sense of these real Alaskan lives. And that feeling has never gone away. So that's what I am hoping, in a small way, to re-create here.

With that in mind, *Only in Florida* is composed of brief stories in the lives of residents that showcase the special qualities of the state, be they alligators, hurricanes, lightning or a Cuban neighborhood. In a place like South Florida, where I live, such a project is almost a necessity. We are the mostly blue tip of a so-called purple state, and many of us haven't been here very long. The majority of us come from places where "interesting" things happened—if you believe the people who tell me they don't have a story down here because they are retired. We come from New York, or Cuba, or Brazil, or elsewhere. According to the U.S. Census Bureau, in 2013–17, 52.9 percent of Miami-Dade residents were foreign-born. And when you factor in all the retirees in Palm Beach County, you've got a massive influx of people who may or may not have a deep knowledge of or commitment to their adopted state. That affects myriad behaviors, from activism and charitable giving to driving and voting.

When it comes to the entire state, the challenge of nonnatives pales—if anything can be pale in the Sunshine State—in comparison to the fact that we are so incredibly diverse in beliefs, interests and experiences. I know quite a few people who see South Florida, for example, as a land of early bird specials (rebranded for baby boomers as sunset specials) and shopping malls. And yet the enormous Sawgrass Mills mall was built on part of the precious, magnificent "river of grass" known as the Everglades. (Which, incidentally, could be one reason why the beloved humorist Dave Barry felt the need to write a book called *Best. State. Ever.: A Florida Man Defends His Homeland.*) We who love Florida do a lot of defending.

Perhaps most significant of all, we are just so big that we affect the national climate. As a quick example, just think of the "hanging chads" incident in the 2000 presidential election. The foibles of one ballot designer and the decision of one supervisor of elections may well have determined the identity of the leader of the free world.

So when it comes to understanding Florida and Floridians, there is a lot to digest, and the stakes are high.

ORAL STORYTELLING

Natives of the Florida Keys often refer to themselves as Conchs, and for good reason: They have been drinking.
—Dave Barry

Now for another few words about oral storytelling. Storytelling, in its purest sense, isn't literature. The root of the word *literature* is related to reading, yet working storytellers tend to think of telling as an oral activity. While I'm not the gatekeeper of the word *storytelling*, and neither is the National Storytelling Network, the professional organization of storytellers, professional storytellers generally know what we all mean by the word. When someone self-identifies as a storyteller first (rather than a writer, or a filmmaker), this person generally works with oral narrative—that is, stories told aloud. And as indicated earlier, prior to writing them down, I heard every one of the stories in this book aloud.

Introduction

Speaking is different than writing in more ways than simply using your mouth rather than your hands. It is more immediate. We learn to create the sounds that comprise words long before we learn to put together the symbols that are letters that comprise words.

Listening is different from reading in more ways than simply using your ears rather than your eyes. It is more immediate. We learn to understand the sounds that comprise words long before we learn to decode the symbols that are letters that comprise words. Our brains process listening faster than they do reading. Ideally, we are, if we put away our phones, looking into the eyes and hearing the voice of the storyteller. We are breathing the same air, experiencing the same energy. We can't go back a sentence or paragraph if we spaced out for a minute. We must be fully present. Listening and being present are skills every bit as valuable in our society as speaking—if not much more so.

Then there is the definition of story itself, at least as I teach it: a causal sequence of events that features at least one character, one setting, one problem and one solution, and result in (a) some sort of transformation, surprising insight or occurrence on the part of the listener and/or main character (protagonist) and (b) an emotional response of some kind on the part of the listener.

What do I mean by a causal sequence of events? The best type of story couldn't really happen any other way. In other words, if you go into a supermarket and grab the last loaf of bread, then decide to get the on-sale milk, then go to the checkout counter and pay, what difference does it make in what order you found the items? But if you picked up the bread first, then on your way to the checkout line happened to see the milk, and the milk container was wet so you dropped it and it opened and poured out all over the bread in your hand, the order matters.

Now you may ask: Well, if the stories were told to you aloud, as you mentioned, and if the spoken word is so important to you, why retell them in your own way? Why not preserve the storyteller's words? The answer is complicated. In short, that would have been a different kind of book. It would have been an anthology of disparate voices, perspectives, grammar and vocabulary, which is lovely, but more of an academic project in some respects. To give a smooth, flowing read, I have chosen to retell the stories in my own voice. I did, however, offer my first drafts to the original storytellers for their input.

Introduction

THE AGE FACTOR

My parents didn't want to move to Florida.
But they turned sixty, and that's the law.
—Jerry Seinfeld

In 2013, the median age in the United States was 37.3. While Florida does not have the highest median age—that honor goes to Maine, at 43.2, about two years more than that of Florida—we certainly have a reputation as a retirement haven. I have had newcomers tell me in surprise that many children live in the state. How else do we make new Floridians? (Oh yes, immigration. Sorry.)

Most, but not all, of the storytellers I've interviewed are middle-aged or senior citizens. Notable exceptions include Joey DeCelles, Alexander Suarez, Diamond-Storm Hosch, Anthony Armonda and my youngest informant, teenager Grace Briden. Again, part of the reason is that these are the people I come across in my daily life and in my audiences. People over sixty make up nearly one-quarter of the state's population, and South Florida reportedly has one of the fastest-growing senior populations in the country. Not only are we all getting older, but Americans still retire to Florida as well. Whatever the cause, according to the *Miami Herald*, Miami-Dade County has the largest number of people over age sixty, and that number will most likely double in the next quarter century—to more than one million.

HABLO INGLÉS

He was of all those things, a bizarre cross-pollination of subcultures
possible only in Florida.
—Ransom Riggs

I have made a considerable effort to highlight the cultural and biodiversity of this great state. First, there are the cultures: Cuban, Seminole, Jamaican, Jewish, African American, Haitian, Greek and more. Then there are the regions. Paradoxically, the farther north you get in Florida, for example, the more you feel like you're in the southern United States. South Florida is populated in large part by Cubans and other Spanish speakers and Caribbean peoples. Plus New Yorkers. Midwesterners, on the other hand, tend to gravitate to the west, or Gulf Coast. Crackers, or native Floridians with many generations of British American ancestors in the state before them, tend to reside in central Florida.

It is this vast diversity that makes our politics and culture so interesting, by the way. For a state known as much for its sugar farmers as its fashion models, I'd say we have done a good job in keeping it together.

SOUTH FLORIDA: AN EXPLANATION

What kind of a person would show up after the Early Bird Special is over? It's unheard of.
—Gregory Bergman and Jodi Miller

I have a confession to make, but you must never tell anyone. More than one-third of the stories in this book take place in South Florida, the region comprising Palm Beach, Broward, Miami-Dade and Monroe Counties. (Some people include the Gulf Coast area of southwestern Florida in this definition, but it is a vastly different place politically and culturally.) In my defense, I am a resident of South Florida. I meet South Floridians every day who regale me with their wonderful stories. In my further defense, as I mentioned above, South Florida is home to many diverse groups who make the region as rich in culture as it is. What is more, I have included only two stories from two cities: Boca Raton, where I live, and Fort Lauderdale, which is, well, Fort Lauderdale. (Yes, Miami and North Miami are two separate cities.) In my further *further* defense, South Florida, aka the Miami metropolitan area, is *huge*. Its population of 6.2 million is a hefty 29 percent of that of the state, at 21.3 million, making it the fourth-most-populated urban area in the nation. In addition, Miami-Dade, Broward and Palm Beach Counties are, respectively, the first, second and third most populous of the state's sixty-seven counties. So yes, we're talking lots of folks. And a lot of stories.

That said, I owe a great debt to Florida Humanities, which has sent me all over the state to tell (and collect) stories as a member of its speakers bureau. Thanks in large part to that wonderful organization, the vast majority of my stories are set outside South Florida.

Introduction

PEOPLE AND THEIR STORIES

Almost everything strange washes up near Miami.
—Rick Riordan

The book is divided into three sections. I am not going to suggest that there isn't overlap among them, such as a story about catching fish in shallow water ("The FlatsMaster") that might well have appeared in the category about animals or about water. I tried to use reasonable criteria for organization, such as: The story is not just about fish; it's about a certain kind of fishing in a boat on a certain kind of water. Whereas a story about crabbing ("Her First Crab") may take place around water, but it's the crabs that are the point; hence, the story belongs with the other animal tales.

I've titled the sections with quotes from the stories because, as I have said, it's people's voices I am primarily interested in. The words we choose matter. I also want to highlight the people who told me and lived the stories I've included. And while we're on the subject, this book could, obviously, not have happened without the fabulous contributions of all the storytellers, professional and amateur, who responded to my call. I only hope that I did them justice.

The first section, "I'm Really Proud of You, Dad": People and Places, begins with a beautiful father/daughter story that humanizes a theme park experience. The section explores the stories that are quintessentially Florida for a variety of reasons: because of the celebrities, encountered in my own first-person account "I Would Only Let Burt Reynolds Do That," and "A Mar-a-Lago Memory," the specific Florida settings ("Harry Potter and the Loving Father," "Elevator to the Shallows," "The Other Side of Paradise"), the situations involving some of our best represented ethnic subcultures ("Help Wanted: Must Farm," "A Bibliothèque in Miami Gardens," "A Jewish Boy in Jacksonville," "Teaching the Holocaust," "Integrating the University of Florida" and "Fakahatchee Archaeology") and, because after all, this is Florida, a portrait in drug crime ("How Much Is Enough?") and "Golf, Of Course."

The second section, "It's a Copper Whopper!": Water and Weather, takes us into the surf in the Gulf of Mexico ("The Sponger and the Seabird," as do the eerily similar "Surfing with Dolphins" and "How One New Yorker Came to Love Florida"), into the flats ("The FlatsMaster"), Biscayne Bay ("Ballast," the first story to include the literary device of a *deus ex machina*, that is, an unexpected life saver) and the wetlands of the Everglades ("Muck in My Moccasins"). It also tells us what happens when you experience the

Introduction

vagaries of Florida weather on the shore, as in "The Costume Must Go On" and "When Lightning Strikes," the second story to feature a seemingly otherworldly savior. And because our hurricanes are essentially who we are in Florida, I include "There's No Place Like Home" and "Why Did the Manatee Cross the Road?"

The third section, "A *Gallo* (Spanish for "rooster") in Miami?": Fauna and Flora, takes its title from one of several stories in the book about, excuse the mixed metaphor, a fish out of water. "The Last *Gringo* in Hialeah" is the tale of a man who never thought he would find a neighbor who would object to a rooster in such a Cuban city. Another theme in this section is the link between humans and animals. "In Dog We Trust," which is not the only time pet therapy appears here, shares that bond with "Hanging with the Gators," "Pelican Urgent Care," "Beating the Blues" and "A Turtle Love Story." There are two stories about trees in this section as well, but they tackle the subject in profoundly different ways. In "The Kite Whisperer," the tree gets the better of the human. In "The Nature of Nature," meanwhile, you might say the trees are also smarter than the humans, but they aren't out to get us. We also find "Aunt Minnie Mae Gets Supper," in which an old-timer shows the kids a thing or two, and "Her First Crab," in which a kid gets what's coming to her—where it hurts.

The story "The Nature of Nature" serves as a fitting wrap-up to the thirty-three stories here, I believe, because it shows that we've been here before, and hopefully, we'll be here again. I like that thought, and I hope you do, too.

STORIES THAT GOT AWAY

*Florida isn't so much a place where one goes to reinvent oneself,
as it is a place where one goes if one no longer wished to be found.*
—Douglas Coupland

Naturally, I couldn't locate a story about every Florida phenomenon. There are, to be exact, gazillions. Some topics I can't believe I missed: early bird specials, flamingos, geckos, jai alai, spring training, tennis and any number of other crucial features of our environment and culture. It's not that they're not interesting; it's just that either I couldn't find the right person or the right story, or I just didn't have space. But trust me, those stories are out there somewhere.

Incidentally, while I made every effort to spread the wealth of stories evenly, some readers may have noticed that the percentage of storytellers identifying as male is relatively low. I find this to be true with our radio segment, as well, and I don't think it is strictly because I am female. It has been suggested by those who study such things that in the general population, men tend to share stories of business, sports and other conquests, while women tend to tell those that are more personal, particularly relating to family and feelings. Perhaps the way I put out the call—asking for true, first-person accounts of quintessentially Florida stories—simply appealed more to women. Or perhaps I'll have to write another book about men's stories. Stay tuned!

FLORIDA'S FUTURE

While living in Florida I realized that I could never stay there, because it's so damn hot. There's only like three months when you don't feel like you're on the cusp of hell.
—*Jennifer L. Armentrout*

According to the U.S. Census Bureau, the rate of newcomers to Florida has tapered off in the last decade or so. While the population is still growing, particularly in the Panhandle (that region to the upper left on the map, that does, in fact, look like a handle), some of the features that made the state such a good location are beginning to wear thin.

Most importantly of all, of course, the air is growing warmer, the hurricanes—though perhaps less frequent—are getting deadlier, and sea level is rising. It's higher and drier in the central and northern parts of the state, but where I am in South Florida, not only are we at about zero feet above sea level but we also are sitting on land that is composed of porous limestone. This means that whether or not there is storm surge—coastal flooding due to rising seas—we're still going to be in trouble. Then there is all that land reclaimed from the Everglades. Question: Why do so many of us living in former swampland have gators in our backyards? Answer: We are in the gators' backyards.

Is this cause for alarm? Certainly. Would most Floridians want to live anywhere else? Not likely. After thirty-five years in the state, with most of that time spent collecting and telling stories of the wonderful people in this amazing place, I can't imagine living anywhere else.

I guess we'll all just have to take our chances. Trust me—paradise is worth it.

Part 1
"I'M REALLY PROUD OF YOU, DAD"

PEOPLE AND PLACES

1
HARRY POTTER AND THE LOVING FATHER

What is there to say about the Walt Disney World Resort and the transformation of land ownership, roads and waterways that it brought to central Florida? Plenty. Located in Lake Buena Vista and Bay Lake, southwest of downtown Orlando, Disney World wasn't technically supposed to happen. According to the *Orlando Weekly*, the genius cartoon mogul Walt Disney had originally planned his "Florida Project" as a rather different park from Disneyland, which he'd built in Anaheim, California, in 1955. Part of his idea for a planned community of the future can be seen in nearby Celebration, Florida. But the rest fell by the wayside after the great man's death in 1966. Instead, Disney World opened its Magic Kingdom in 1971, and Epcot, Hollywood Studios and the Animal Kingdom appeared over the next few decades. Today, more than fifty million people have visited Mickey Mouse, making the attraction the planet's most popular vacation destination, with seventy-four thousand employees—and I would wager an eager applicant is born every minute.

This story isn't actually about Disney World, however. It's about a nearby theme park that tourists usually pair with Disney, Universal Orlando Resort. And you can be sure that Universal wouldn't exist without the transformation wrought by Walt Disney and his brother Roy nearly five decades ago. Founded in 1990, Universal features all things motion picture, including its blockbuster Harry Potter and the Escape from Gringotts™. Says its website:

"See goblins hard at work. Then, get ready to take a journey through cavernous passageways that lead deep underground as you climb aboard this mind-blowing, multi-dimensional thrill ride.…You'll have to evade the wrath of malicious villains…as well as trolls and other creatures that stand between you and a safe return."

The Universal Orlando Resort was founded in 1990. David Sinofsky, freeimages.com.

Get the picture?

Anyway, this story takes us on a different kind of journey. It's about what we do for our children—and the lengths (and widths) to which we go in order to fit in. Sometimes literally.

WHEN DR. BILL TRAPANI moved his small family to Florida from Detroit in 2009, he was looking forward to more than a change in university faculty positions. He was conscious of relocating from the car-centric city he had lived in as a younger man to a more active lifestyle. Just one look at the perky seniors race-walking through the malls convinced him that he was in a whole different world. Sure, Florida's nickname is "The Sunshine State." But for him, it looked more like the "Slim-down State."

Not that everybody here was exactly pinup material. But most of the folks he saw looked a whole lot better than he knew he did. He had struggled with his weight most of his life, yo-yoing up and down the scale, mostly down while in grad school. But now, at about 335 pounds, he had reached a new personal record. And man, was he uncomfortable lugging all that weight around the humid Florida parking lots.

Hardest of all at his present weight was caring for his two-year-old daughter, Ellie. Sure, she had a mom. But she also wanted Daddy to go to the park. She wanted Daddy to help her ride a tricycle. She wanted Daddy to play. Unfortunately, keeping up with her was tougher for Bill than defending his doctoral dissertation. It felt more like winning the Nobel Prize. Twice.

Speaking of which, have you noticed they grow Harry Potter fans younger and younger these days? He barely realized his daughter could read when he realized that she had somehow gotten into Harry Potter in a big way. The books were just a small part, of course. There were the

"I'm Really Proud of You, Dad": People and Places

movies. The action figures. The bed sheets and pajamas. And yes, the ride at Universal Studios in Orlando.

Ellie Trapani was about six when the theme park installed the Harry Potter rides. And hers was one of the first families to visit it. At the time, however, she was too short to go on the ride she really wanted: Harry Potter and the Forbidden Journey, a roller coaster with an unobstructed view of Hogwarts Castle.

No fan of the boy wizard himself, Bill remembers all this as if it were yesterday because, well, his daughter wouldn't stop talking about it. He even looked it up online. He learned that the Forbidden Journey is not, technically, a roller-coaster ride. By way of special "robocoaster" technology, the seats on the "scenic dark ride" swivel above the track, held in place by a robotic arm. *Only a tech wizard could make that up*, he reflected.

At last, Ellie announced to her parents that she had reached the posted height requirement of forty-eight inches. She had long ago learned the magic number, and the Trapanis had in fact more than once used it as an incentive to induce her to eat a more balanced diet. If all else failed, she told them the night before the big trip, she could tease up her hair a bit. Whatever it took, she was determined to make it work.

"Besides," she assured her dad before drifting off to sleep, "I'll be taller tomorrow."

The morning of the big adventure arrived. Bill kissed his wife good-bye at the door. Then he turned to his little girl.

"Okay," he said. "Let's do it!"

They made the three-hour drive in good time, but as any denizen of Disney knows, it's the line that takes patience. Universal was no different. Finally, they were about ten minutes from the front. Even Bill could feel his anticipation rising. He felt the little hand squeezing his pinkie finger for all it was worth.

It was then that a young attendant approached him. The kid couldn't have been more than eighteen, and he seemed to wear his authority with as much discomfort as he did his stiff-looking uniform.

"Excuse me, sir," he said. "Would you come over here for a minute?" Bill didn't want to lose his hard-won place in line, but the guy was pointing to a chair that looked like a replica of one that might be on the ride.

Bill looked down at Ellie. She looked up at him. At the same time, they shrugged.

"Sure," he said. *Must be they want a funny picture*, he thought. *I'll bet they pull every thousandth tourist out of line and give him a souvenir.*

Then he realized what was happening. Like his daughter had experienced before, he was being measured for the ride. But far from trying to stretch to fit, he found himself desperately trying to pull the bar down over his belly. The more he tried, the more of a challenge it became. He simply could not tuck himself in, no matter how he squirmed. Bill felt a familiar rivulet of sweat snake down his brow, but this time, it wasn't from the Florida heat. He felt his heart begin to pound with embarrassment.

At last the attendant spoke up. "I'm really sorry, sir," he said, shaking his head. "But you can't go on the ride if you can't pull down the safety bar. It's the law."

Bill climbed out of the chair and reached for his daughter's hand. Clearly, she didn't understand. Why were they leaving the line, when they had stood there for so long and gotten so close to the front? What was going on?

When they were well away from the ride, Bill knelt down beside his little girl.

"Honey," he said. "You fit into the seat now, but Daddy doesn't. I'm too big."

"Can I go on myself?" she asked, not missing a beat.

"Sorry, no. But we'll come again when I lose some weight. I promise, baby. We'll come again really, really soon."

The drive home felt like the longest of his life. Neither father nor daughter talked a lot. They had tried a few other attractions at the park, but neither of them had the heart for them. And when it came to lunch, Bill, ironically, perhaps, had no appetite.

He was devastated. It was one thing to have fellow passengers look at him with fear when he approached their seat on a plane—or just as bad, to appear invisible to strangers. He'd come to terms with who he was and what he looked like, and it had never bothered him much. But to see himself in his daughter's eyes—and to disappoint her like that—was a whole different experience. This was true motivation to change.

There was no Harry Potter magic to what Bill did next. He dieted. He walked. He attended Weight Watchers meetings and made a good friend with whom he regularly went on hikes. By the following year, he'd lost 130 pounds.

Once again, father and daughter drove to Universal. They rode the Harry Potter ride. Twice. After the second go-round, Ellie looked up at him and smiled.

"I'm really proud of you, Dad," she said.

He squeezed her shoulder. "I'm always proud of you, honey."

After that, they each bought an ice cream.

"We can have this, right, Daddy?" she asked, holding up her chocolate cone.

"We absolutely can," Bill assured her. "We can have anything we want."

2
I WOULD ONLY LET BURT REYNOLDS DO THAT

I've performed this story several times for audiences, along with a much longer section about the cost of fame, complete with tabloid photos and headlines—the only time I have ever used visual aids—about the man I've come to think of as "poor, maligned, misunderstood Burt Reynolds." Somehow, I don't think my audiences ever see him the same way I do. And I am *quite* sure the great man himself never did. One thing's for certain: his picture should stand beside the word *charisma* in the dictionary.

I doubt that many of us like to think of ourselves as starstruck. At least no one who has ever spent a fair amount of time in New York or LA, as I have. Over the years, I've crossed paths with such luminaries as the playwright Lillian Hellman, exercise king Richard Simmons, sexologist Dr. Ruth, pop singer Carly Simon, *Saturday Night Live* comedian Bill Murray, movie actors Shirley MacLaine and Mark Ruffalo, among others. These were certainly not what you would call relationships; they were celebrity sightings punctuated by perhaps a shared glance, a smile or at most a few words. But as much as I hate to admit it, child of television and the movies that I am, I was thrilled every time.

Then there was Burt Reynolds. You have to remember Burt Reynolds. He was the dark-haired 1970s-era mustachioed heartthrob with the messy divorce from TV sex symbol Loni Anderson. He was the nude centerfold in *Cosmopolitan* magazine. His TV and film appearances were, among a certain segment of the population, at least, legendary. *Gunsmoke. Smokey and the Bandit. The Cannonball Run. Deliverance*, which could have

Burt Reynolds wasn't acting when he played football for Florida State University. *State Archives of Florida.*

won an Oscar, it was said, if not for that centerfold. *Evening Shade*. Box office gold. *That* Burt Reynolds.

For South Floridians, Mr. Reynolds is a local boy. True, he was actually born in Michigan, but he grew up in South Florida's Riviera Beach, the wayward son of a local cop. And he got his big acting break at Palm Beach Community College after injuring himself out of a football career.

At times it seems like everyone around here has a Burt Reynolds story. For a while, he owned a theater in Jupiter, and he gave acting classes. Then he sort of disappeared from the scene, at least as far as I knew—until, that is, the spring of 2003.

I was just finishing up a graduate program at Florida Atlantic University in Boca Raton and in the midst of a career in writing and storytelling. I was set to teach at the university in the fall. I had purchased tickets to fly to New York for a family occasion when, to my shock, I came across a flyer—I have no idea how, for all I know it fell from the sky—offering acting classes at the Burt Reynolds & Friends Museum in Jupiter. Taught by the big man himself.

"I'm Really Proud of You, Dad": People and Places

Now, I hadn't even known there *was* a Burt Reynolds & Friends Museum. What's more, the fee was higher than I could reasonably afford, and it was for eight three-hour evening classes spread over three weeks. But I felt like I needed a treat, especially one that could quite possibly help my performance career. At least that's what I told myself. In reality, I was just starstruck.

When I looked more closely at the flyer, however, my heart sank. Three of the classes took place while I was scheduled to be up north. Somehow, I couldn't bring myself to throw out the flyer, however. And it was a good thing I didn't. Because a week before I was set to leave, my husband tore a ligament, and I had to stay home to care for him.

Luckily, I didn't need to be with him twenty-four hours a day. I pulled out the flyer and decided that since the classes were at night, my husband could do without me for a few evenings. I sent in the application form and *abracadabra*, as we say in show business, I was in, and I was thrilled. I figured it was the closest to belonging to the real Hollywood (as opposed to Hollywood, Florida) as I was going to get. They even sent me a little monologue to memorize for the first session.

When the first evening of class arrived, I was surprised to find that the "museum" was a room and a half on the ground floor of a small, drab-looking office building at the sleepy corner of Indiantown Road and U.S. 1 in Jupiter. In the parking lot, I joined a couple dozen mostly younger people milling about. We entered when the doors opened and approached a table, behind which stood a rather stern, platinum-haired woman I came to know as Pam, the former cocktail waitress who was at the time Mr. Reynolds's fiancée. (I never called him anything, by the way, but if I had, "Mr. Reynolds" seems appropriate.) She took our checks, and we moved into the first of the museum's rooms, to the folding chairs facing a tall director's chair in the middle of a small riser, or temporary stage. Murmuring to one another, we gaped at the movie posters and bits of memorabilia from his career exhibited around the room. Was this *it*?

And then he walked in, wearing an electric-blue sweatshirt and looking, frankly, like a wax approximation of a movie star. Seventy-two years and plastic surgery, I reflected, had not been good to Burt Reynolds. But those thoughts melted away as he began to talk. (Actually, he had me at his smile hello.) I know a lot of storytellers, but never have I encountered such a wonderful raconteur. Over the next three weeks, he talked about taking acting classes with Marilyn Monroe sitting shyly in the back row. He talked about the two great loves of his life, Sally Field and Dinah Shore. He told a memorable story about how the director of his hit movie *Deliverance* got the actor Ned Beatty to honestly fear his on-screen rapist. (By running naked alongside his car on filming day.)

Of course, he also told us a lot about the craft of acting in sessions that ran way past the scheduled three-hour cutoff to three and four o'clock in the morning. He complimented me on my first monologue and gave me a scene to do with him, although ultimately I was too nervous to learn my lines and did something else instead. We studied with his celebrity friends Bruce Dern and Charles Nelson Reilly, the latter of whom was, for some unaccountable reason, fairly nasty to most of what I thought of as the "real" acting students but amazingly sweet to me.

Over the weeks, several students spent a fair amount of time chatting with Mr. Reynolds during break, or taking pictures, but I said very little to him. I didn't want to seem to take advantage. I also respected his privacy, apparently, much more than he did. Or maybe I was just nervous.

Despite the late nights, the course passed quickly. In preparation for our final "graduation" showcase, we were each given a scene to do with another student. My partner was supposed to be a jailed criminal; I was a shy, innocent girl who was attracted to him. In his notes to me after we rehearsed the scene, Mr. Reynolds said I needed to be more shy and innocent. I responded that I'd worked for decades to lose those very qualities, and it wasn't easy to get them back. He laughed a lot at that. He told me I needed to do some "business" with my hands, so I grabbed a knife and apple from the refreshment bar, which led him to chide me for waving a knife around a convict. I kept forgetting my lines, to the mild frustration of not only him but also my scene partner. Yet the star was always patient, always mindful that I was in fact a storyteller, not an actor.

And then came the big night of the show, to which we were each allowed to invite a couple of guests. My aunt and uncle sat beaming in the back. At last my partner and I were called to the stage, and somehow, I got through the scene in one piece and reveled in the applause.

As I climbed down the riser to return to my seat, I felt what my grandmother used to call a *potch*: a smack on my backside. I wheeled around—it was years before #MeToo, but nevertheless, who had the nerve to do that to me in public? And then I saw who it was. His handsome eyes twinkled, and he smiled broadly under the graying moustache.

"Good work, kid," he said.

I smiled back. "You know, I don't even let my husband or my father do that," I said. "I would only let you." I think my words surprised me a lot more than they did him.

"I'm Really Proud of You, Dad": People and Places

Some time later, along with a few other students, I volunteered to speak at a town hall meeting to try to get funding to save the museum, but the attempt ultimately failed. The last time I saw Burt Reynolds was a decade later, at a special event in a little theater in nearby Stuart, at which they were showing a film he had directed in the seventies, and he was scheduled to make an appearance. He had been so accessible years before that I was really expecting to be able to speak to him, imagining, even, that he would remember me. This time, however, he was seated on the stage at intermission and interviewed by the moderator with questions the standing-room-only audience had prepared in advance. At the time over eighty, he was still funny, smart and charming, but somehow already beginning to disappear. I was sad to see a ghost of that vital man I'd known for a very little while and sadder still to know that he wouldn't likely be around much longer.

But I still would have let him smack my butt.

3
THE OTHER SIDE OF PARADISE

The economic center of Florida's west coast, Tampa is one of the most desirable places to live in the state. It tends to skew professional and fairly progressive. The public schools are above average. Tourist attractions like Busch Gardens draw in visitors from around the world. Life is generally good.

Three million people live in Tampa, and about one out of every ten of them—plus tourists—turns up at the Parade of Pirates, the crown jewel of the annual Gasparilla Pirate Festival, held each January. The parade, considered the third largest in the nation, with an annual economic impact to the city of $22 million, celebrates, like the festival itself, the treacherous career of the Spanish pirate José Gaspar. Gasparilla, or "Little Gaspar," as he called himself, may or may not have existed, and if he did, he may or may not have lived in the late eighteenth and early nineteenth centuries. But one thing is pretty clear: He almost certainly never fought a battle in Tampa Bay around 1821.

Such petty details are of little concern to the revelers, however. Starting at Bay and Bayshore Boulevards, the 4.5-mile parade route ends at the corner of Cass Street and Ashley Drive. And according to my former student Alexander Suarez, it is much more than just a parade. It is a celebration of color and sound and history and youth and—on second thought, it's a parade, all right. One of the best. Meanwhile, offshore, hundreds of boats converge on Tampa Bay alongside the marchers' route. At some point, the

"I'm Really Proud of You, Dad": People and Places

The Gasparilla Festival celebrates a dastardly, and possibly fictional, Spanish pirate—all in good fun. *State Archives of Florida.*

mayor even gives the keys of the city to the year's stand-in for José Gaspar. Sounds odd, maybe, but then who can argue with tradition?

Alex posted his impressions of his part in the spectacle on his blog, but we also met after class one evening to discuss the story further. A nontraditional college student—that is, considerably more mature, with years of experience in the work world behind him—Alex was extremely enthusiastic about his education, about Florida and about the future. This story details a small slice of the life of a man with big dreams.

"Hands in the air for beads!" DJ Carlos screamed out to the growing crowd. And the paradegoers, mostly young and mostly inebriated, happily complied. Greedily they reached for the multicolored Mardi Gras beads flung out from the floats, preferring the largest and those coated in the brightest shades of gold.

Alex Suarez stood on the yellow-and-blue Hillsborough Community College float, reaching down to hand out the biggest beads he could grab from his stash.

"Who wants it?" he called to the army of flashing heads and limbs. "Hands in the air!"

Sometimes it took a few tries to send the strands to the prettiest women in the crowd, but Alex could usually hit his target if he really tried. Friends cried out to him too, but he only learned that later. He didn't notice them in the clamor.

Alex was a student at Hillsborough Community College in Ybor City, in the middle of Tampa's historic Latin quarter. Like every large city, greater Tampa has its array of neighborhoods. Northeast of downtown, Ybor City was founded by cigar manufacturers and serves as home to Cuban, Spanish and Italian immigrants. Its standard of living has risen and fallen over the years, in part due to demand for its products. It is very much a working-class neighborhood.

Like community colleges everywhere, HCC caters to local students, often those who work and have families to support, with more energy than money and more bills than time. Not far away looms the sprawling main campus of the University of South Florida, which boasts fifty thousand students. There is also Tampa University. Though much smaller than USF, it is a private school that costs its undergraduates upward of $40,000 a year in tuition and fees.

As with townies and rich imports in any college town, there is always a certain amount of friction between the two groups. It doesn't usually erupt into anything tangible; but there is no getting around it. The Tampa U students look down on the locals. Sometimes they shout taunts out of car windows or mutter slurs as they pass on the street. And the locals, particularly the HCC kids, hate it.

"I'm Really Proud of You, Dad": People and Places

Alex had felt the slights, and depending on his mood, they could really get to him. But he had troubles of his own. There wasn't much money at home, and he was dependent on scholarships and part-time jobs to afford tuition.

But today was different. Today, it was Alex who looked down on everyone, at least literally. Like him, the other student government and club representatives on the float were taking time from work, or from their studies, or from their families, but the sacrifice was well worth it. For those few hours, whether it was their turn to ride the float or—to keep the weight down for security reasons—walking several miles beside it, they were gods. And the beads were their gifts to their worshippers.

Alex was in the middle of his shift on the float when an especially loud, intoxicated voice rose up from the crowd.

"Hey you, give 'em here!"

He turned around to face the living, breathing image of his nemesis: a tan, blond, muscle-bound guy dressed in a red-and-black Tampa University T-shirt and baggy white shorts, with a long-haired, half-naked coed on each arm.

"Beads!" the girls screeched up at him. "Please, please, give us beads!"

Maybe it was the sun. Maybe it was the beer (although he had none on the float, he saw plenty of beer in the crowd) or the general excitement of the day. Whatever the reason, Alex had never felt so powerful in his life. At that moment, he forgot he was on a float in a parade that would end in an hour or two. He forgot that the beads were virtually worthless and that these kids could purchase bags of them any day of the week. All he could think of was that they wanted something from him. They *really* wanted something from him, and he had the power to grant or deny it. At long last the Ybor students like him were the ones with the power.

In the distance, he could hear the floats reenacting the pirate invasion of Tampa Harbor. He could feel the crowds streaming from every direction. He could practically smell the sweat that snaked down every face and spine.

For what might have been a full minute, Alex stood staring at the shining trio of students, beads pouring down his arms. He thought of his dad, most likely sitting in front of the TV. He thought of the hours he himself put in each week making tuition and rent. He thought of how he would soon have to climb down off the float and once again join his place among the mortals. Then he thought of where he was going in life: on stage, in print, on the Net, into the big time. Far from this place.

And then he lifted the ropes of beads high above his head. As he did so, he watched the eyes of the three students grow wide, as if there were no one else on the street. Then, with all his might, Alex threw the colorful strands in their direction. The beads landed in the students' open hands as if they'd had wings. Before they turned around to the next distraction, the guy saluted him. Man to man.

At last the float reached downtown, and Alex and his cohort made one last pitch to the crowd. Then, just as he was thinking he had nothing more to give, the DJ handed him the microphone. It was an opportunity that Alex, a student reporter, could not forego.

"Ybor City, represent!" he shouted over the blaring rock music. And the crowd, if possible, went just a little crazier, dancing and screaming and scrambling for still more beads.

Sometime later, Alex returned to the small rental he shared with his father, utterly exhausted. He looked around at the simple surroundings, reached into the refrigerator and grabbed a beer. Settling down on the worn couch next to his dad, he paused to take stock. Maybe he no longer felt like a god, but he sure felt a little more like a king.

4

A JEWISH BOY IN JACKSONVILLE

By 1928, about 40 percent of the state's Jewish population resided in Jacksonville. Today, at fifteen thousand, that number is about 2 percent. Although Jacksonville is the site of Florida's first Jewish institution—the Jacksonville Hebrew Cemetery, established in 1857—writer/researcher Arlo Haskell claims that the city has a history of anti-Semitism, at least in the early years of the twentieth century. Maybe that's because, located as it is less than fifty miles from the Georgia border, "First Coast," as the city is called, has much of the feel, and the population, of the Deep South. And while there are certainly Jewish communities in Alabama, Atlanta and elsewhere, we tend to associate Dixie more with chitlins (a staple of soul food) than with cholent (an Eastern European Jewish dish).

I've known storyteller Eva Cohen for close to twenty years, but only within the last few did she become a Jacksonville resident. Like most recent transplants from the Northeast, Eva and her husband, Arthur, had certain preconceptions about this great purple state of ours. And like many Jews, if they had been asked, they might have said that South Florida, which has the largest concentration of Jews outside of Israel, would welcome them with open arms. In Florida, however, the farther north you go, the more southern the people are. As this story demonstrates, you never know what to expect.

THE COHENS SPENT MUCH of their married life in a six-bedroom home in Pennsylvania, in a small city about seventy miles west of New York City. Eva is the descendant of a revered Jewish historian. She grew up attending

Only in Florida

Eva and Arthur Cohen left New Jersey for Jacksonville and never looked back.
Courtesy of Eva and Arthur Cohen.

a religious day school, but though her family was considered Orthodox, her parents did not observe many of the commandments, including driving on the Sabbath and eating shellfish. It wasn't until she was hired to tell Bible stories as an adult, in fact, that Eva truly came to appreciate her religion.

Arthur, meanwhile, comes from a family of *kohayns*, meaning he is a descendant of Aaron, the first Jewish priest at the Holy Temple in Jerusalem, a status that affords him certain privileges in the synagogue. That doesn't mean he is an observant man either—far from it. He knows his prayers and can recite them at synagogue, but as for holiday observances and keeping kosher, he can take them or leave them. And he generally leaves them.

A few years after their children moved out of the house, the couple decided it was time to downsize. They had good friends who had resettled in Florida from Honolulu, and they began to visit them in their new home in Ponte Vedra Beach, in northeast Florida. Soon they were talking real estate, and they proceeded to go house-hunting with their friends' realtor.

It wasn't long before they found the perfect place: a condo on the beach in Jacksonville, less than a thirty-minute drive from their friends' home. The realtor assured them that the beautiful view would never change, because the height of the buildings theirs overlooked could not by law be taller than three stories—unless grandfathered in, which none of them was. They were within a short walk from restaurants, the cleaners and the tennis courts. And most important to them, the building was not occupied by snowbirds, those temporary residents from elsewhere who poured in only in the winter months. Those few who didn't remain there throughout the year lived nearby and used the condo as their weekend beach home. Thus the place would have the feeling of a neighborhood, a community, all year long.

"I'm Really Proud of You, Dad": People and Places

At last they had the lifestyle they had longed for. All amenities included. All needs anticipated. They looked at each other that first evening in the apartment and, not for the first time, read each other's thoughts. *We will be here for the rest of our lives, if all goes well. It doesn't get any better than this.*

The couple knew that less than 10 percent of the building's residents were Jewish, unlike South Florida, where a condo community might be less than 10 percent *non*-Jewish. But they didn't know much else about the demographics. Eva traveled a fair amount for work, but Arthur was retired. Because he was around so much, he got to know some of the neighbors. And it wasn't long before conversations about garbage pickup and kids turned to improvements they could make in their community. And for that, he and Eva needed to attend a meeting of the condo association.

The couple listened intently at their first meeting, following the agenda items with the enthusiasm of newcomers eager to learn. When they were asked to stand and introduce themselves, they did so with all the aplomb of children starting a new school year.

So Arthur and Eva were feeling good as they stood up after the meeting and walked over to the refreshment table. They spotted the neighbor who had invited them standing in a small group by the door.

Before Arthur could pour his coffee, however, a small, dark-haired man in his early seventies approached him. Eva had noticed his attractive wife sitting next to him at the table.

The man grinned. "Hey, fella!" he said to Arthur, in a honeyed drawl. "I wanna ask you something! Are you a Jewish boy?"

Here it comes, Eva thought, looking at her normally relaxed husband grit his teeth. *We knew it was too good to be true.* Anti-Semitism, and they had just moved in! Why hadn't they moved to South Florida after all, where everyone told them they'd fit right in among half a million of their kind?

"Excuse me?" her husband said, drawing himself up to his full height. She could tell he was intentionally making his voice a little edgier, a little tougher than usual.

"I asked," the man repeated, moving closer, "are you a Jewish boy? I heard you introduce yourselves as Cohens, and I was just wondering."

"Yes, yes I am," Arthur said. Then he repeated the question back to the man, mockingly imitating the man's strong southern twang.

"Are *you* a Jewish boy?" It was the only thing he could think of to say.

To his surprise, the man grinned broadly.

"Yes I am! How would you and your wife like to join us at the Beaches Synagogue Friday night?"

Arthur hadn't realized that his shoulders had tensed up to his ears until he felt them drop with relief. He smiled broadly, clapped the man on the back and shook his hand.

"The name's Sidney," the man said. "Pleased to meet you."

"I'm Arthur, and this is Eva. Cohen. But then you already know that."

After Sabbath services at the synagogue that Friday evening, Sidney and his wife, Sharon, introduced Eva and Arthur to their favorite Italian restaurant. Through Sharon, Eva met other Jewish women and became progressively more involved in local Jewish activities. And the four have been friendly ever since. Forever after, when they laugh about this story, the couples reflect that it is just one more chapter in the ever-surprising history of the Jews.

5
ELEVATOR TO THE SHALLOWS

There's a classic French thriller called *Elevator to the Gallows*, based on a novel of the same name, in which a supposedly perfect murder is exposed due to the hero's entrapment in an elevator. While that may be a little extreme a comparison for this story—because for one thing the "crimes" committed here were of the soul rather than of the gun—nonetheless, the tale reminds us that older doesn't always mean wiser. Or kinder. Not to mention the fact that elevators can cause trouble. Still, the tale features at least one real-life hero. And *that* reminds us that good people can be found in any population.

I hadn't yet met or corresponded with Sol "Isidore" Friedman when I came across his elevator story. He had contributed "Elevators That Changed Kings Point" to a privately published volume called *The View From Kings Point: The Kings Point Writers Club Anthology, 2018*, edited by Edward R. Levenson. When I looked through the book for "only in Florida" stories, this one was almost too perfect. It has it all: a senior-only neighborhood, "condo commandos" (seniors who wield power in their over-sixty-five communities) and a hero well past his sixty-fifth birthday. In fact, about the only thing it's missing is an early bird special. Excuse me. We call them twilight suppers now.

I think my favorite thing about the story, though, is that retirees are always telling me that all their good stories happened "up north," before they retired to South Florida. Yet here is an example of a man who never stopped making a difference.

In the swim at Kings Point in Delray Beach. *The Kings Points Recreation Corporation Inc.*

KING POINT IS A retirement community located in Delray Beach, a small city in south Palm Beach County, on the southeast coast of the state. When fully occupied, the community's 7,200 one- and two-bedroom condominiums house approximately 15,000 "active adults" (read: fifty-five-plus, *sans* children) who are able to play shuffleboard and billiards on site, work out, swim in the indoor and outdoor pools, enjoy shows in the large auditorium and, most importantly, enjoy life, notes kingspointdelray.com. Apartment prices range from a low of about $40,000 to a high of $167,000. In other words, this is not the high-rent district of the county; rather, it is well within the price range of its overwhelmingly white, lower-middle-class residents.

It's a little odd to think that such a place would ever have a fair number of two-story buildings without elevators, and yet, such was the case in this story. Presumably, top-floor residents who stayed long enough to need a lift migrated down to ground-floor housing or simply switched communities altogether.

Enter Sol Friedman. It was January 1992. Sol had just returned from a business trip to Egypt when his neighbor Millie Flam accosted him by the mailboxes. A new board member for Normandy N—units are clustered in alphabetically located enclaves, each of which has its own sub-clusters named for letters of the alphabet—he had come to expect neighbors' demands. What he hadn't bargained for was the board president's resignation soon after, at which point Sol was asked to step in. And the demands, shall we say, elevated.

"See what you can do to get an elevator for our condo," Millie said, brandishing a circular for Kmart like a miniature sword. Millie was thin and angular, a determined woman in her mid-seventies. She had a reputation for speaking her mind, particularly when it was something to do with her or her husband.

"Jack can't get up and down the steps anymore," she continued. "It isn't right."

It seemed to Sol like a simple enough request. Not only did he want to do what was best for the community, but as an engineer, he liked to solve problems. The distance from the first floor to the second was just ten feet, but it might as well have been ten miles for a man with a disability.

Sol Friedman was, you should excuse the expression, an idealist. He hadn't been on Florida condo boards long enough to know how they worked. Like anywhere else in the halls of power, a lot occurs behind closed doors, even in the Sunshine State, with its aptly named Sunshine Law mandating open government.

Like any good public servant, Sol talked to his constituency. It soon became apparent to him that the first-floor occupants, led, incidentally, by the former board president, wanted nothing less than an elevator for the convenience of their upstairs neighbors. The building process would be a mess. The elevator would take up room. People would congregate by it and make noise, leave garbage or worse. Besides, that second-floor crowd knew what they were getting into when they moved in, didn't they? Not to mention the health benefits of climbing stairs! Some people paid good money to go to a gym to do that! Didn't *they* wish they had free stairs to climb every day? But you didn't hear *them* complaining!

Sol talked to a number of his friends in the community, as well as insurance people. It was clear to him that using the stairs on a regular basis could be hazardous to the health of some of the seniors in the community. But no one with a say in the matter came forward to support him. And unless a majority of the homeowners in the building agreed to pay for an elevator, it wasn't going to happen.

What would it take to convince them? Sol wondered aloud to his wife, Henny. A tragic accident?

At the next meeting of the Normandy N Board of Directors, he stood up.

"I think we need to get some legal advice," he told his colleagues. "It could cost some money, but this is our responsibility." The board agreed, and an attorney was hired.

Some $3,000 later, the upshot was this: Unless a majority of the homeowners in the building wanted to pay for an elevator, it wasn't going to happen. As they already knew $3,000 earlier. So what was a good man to do? Sol reached out to government agencies and found a friendly employee in the Tallahassee Office of the Elderly. She suggested he research amendments to the federal Civil Rights Acts. In other words, there had to be a law to protect Jack Flam.

So it was that Sol found himself pulling his car into the parking lot of the stately Florida Atlantic University Library on Glades Road, an eight-mile drive from the site of the Elevator Debacle.

And debacle it was. Because the more questions Sol asked, the angrier the first-floor residents got at those on the second floor, and vice versa. Neighbors stopped talking to neighbors. Friends broke up longstanding card games. It got to the point that just about the only folks safe from the first-floor residents' ire were the owners of the two second-floor units who lived approximately four hundred feet away from the proposed lift. They had no intention of paying for an elevator, either. What good would it do them, on the other end of the hall? Which meant, by the way, that they weren't too popular with the condo owners on *their* floor.

Anyway, thanks to a university research librarian and a heart full of patience, Sol finally found the amendment he was after. According to the 1998 Fair Housing Amendment: "Anyone who is handicapped may make such changes to a public dwelling that would result in an improvement to his living."

And what were these handicaps? Physical impairment. Emphysema. Drug addiction. Tuberculosis. Alcoholism. Plus any other physical or mental handicap.

This was the language he was looking for. Here was his case.

Almost overnight, Sol transformed from president to general. He marshaled his troops on the second floor to get doctors' letters describing in detail their physical ailments. At that meeting, ten people raised their hands, agreeing to obtain the necessary documentation.

Millie delivered Jack's letter that same week. Sol waited for the other nine homeowners to come through.

And he waited. And he waited. But none of his cajoling, none of his wife's sit-downs with the wives, could get the others to commit.

But the law said "anyone," and that meant any *one*. So Sol took Jack's lone statement with him to file a discrimination complaint with the State of Florida. Now he had to wait again, this time for the time allowed by law for the state to reply before the complaint could be forwarded to the federal authorities.

Meanwhile, Sol, who knew a winning cause when he saw it, began to solicit bids from contractors. This too was a learning experience. Three-phase current was necessary to power the elevator, adding $4,000 to the $56,000-plus price tag. Divided by twenty-four apartments on the second floor, that would come to over $2,500 a unit. Not to mention the expense of maintenance. It was going to be a hard sell, but Sol kept his fingers crossed.

The board of directors met once more. Sol made an impassioned speech, and the hands rose in favor. But when it came to forking over the cash, there were still two holdouts out of the twenty-four on the second floor. Not to mention the fact that the first-floor owners still didn't want the elevator built, either. Even if they didn't have to pay for it.

It was two years after the original filing that Sol opened the letter telling him that now the matter was in the hands of the federal Housing and Urban Development Agency. Again Sol waited. At last, HUD informed him that he should try to use arbitration to reach some sort of agreement with the first-floor owners.

Two years passed, and several attempts at arbitration failed. Now the problem sat on the desk of U.S. Attorney General Janet Reno. The AG signed an order allowing the elevator to be built and assigned an attorney to the case to make it happen.

But the story was still not over. The original plan was for the elevator to be located in the middle of the building. The first-floor residents there would not allow the elevator near their homes. Now it was the turn of a Miami judge, who eventually determined that the lift would be located at the end of the building.

Millie Flam didn't live on the end of the building, but she agreed, just so the matter would be settled. And thus the elevator became a reality in 1998—six years after Sol's initial filing.

But the story was still not over. Three or four years passed, and the maintenance of the elevator was costing the second floor an arm and a leg. The first-floor owners finally agreed to share the costs. In addition, the insurance company kicked in $10,000 due to the condo association's failure to build the elevator.

Was Jack Flam happy? Who knows? Poor Jack died from complications of diabetes well before the elevator ever carried its first passenger.

6

INTEGRATING THE UNIVERSITY OF FLORIDA

Kitty Oliver, PhD, is a woman of many talents. Oral historian, international consultant on race and diversity, jazz singer, author, academic, journalist—any of these professions would be enough for one person, but she has done it all. And more remarkably still, she did it as an African American woman, despite having grown up in Florida at a time when the mighty University of Florida—like so many institutions in the nation—was profoundly racist.

I have known and admired Kitty for twenty years or so, since our paths crossed first as students, and then as professors, at Florida International and Florida Atlantic University. I own her memoir, *Multicolored Memoirs of a Black Southern Girl*. But there is nothing like hearing someone's story, which is what I was recently able to do. Here is my retelling.

In 1965, one year after the passage of the Civil Rights Act, the University of Florida in Gainesville, flagship of the state university system and founded nearly a decade before the start of the Civil War, was obliged to integrate. That year, the university allowed in five black freshmen among its student population of eighteen thousand. One of these was Kitty Oliver, age seventeen, from Jacksonville.

The other four black freshmen were (1) a girl Kitty knew in high school who kept to herself and soon left college, (2) her "randomly selected" roommate and (3, 4) two boys from Miami. Kitty was glad they would be

"I'm Really Proud of You, Dad": People and Places

Dr. Kitty Oliver is an academic, author, jazz singer, journalist, oral historian and more. *candacewest.com*.

there with her because she hadn't had any real contact with white people back home. But she hadn't been afraid to leave, either. The discomfort of being different couldn't compete with her discomfort at the prospect of staying home. Kitty had always loved movies and TV, observing how the people on the screen lived. Now, she would have a chance to observe them firsthand—and even to play a role in the story.

"Aren't you afraid?" her friends and family members asked her. "What if it's dangerous? Anything could happen!"

"I'm different from you in that way," she replied. "The possibility of going into something new, something strange, even if it might be dangerous—that's an adventure. That's what I'm drawn to."

The university prepared the black students by warning them that the school could only protect them in areas over which it had control. If they went into downtown Gainesville, or even up the street from campus, university officials couldn't say what would happen. They were true to their word, too.

And so, never leaving campus, Kitty was never afraid for her safety. What she encountered that first week was, however, nearly as disturbing as physical assault. She left her dorm room that first day with a sense of possibility. What she encountered instead was—nothing. She was totally ignored, as if she were invisible. It was an assault not on her person, but rather on her spirit. It hurt so badly, in fact, that she realized she needed to guard her emotions, to psychologically shield herself before making her way through the thousands of students on the tree-lined campus or walking into enormous classrooms. She consciously set up a barrier, a protective coating to help her handle the pain that the students' indifference was causing her. With all that she had anticipated about this move, she had never considered this.

Kitty's roommate came from Titusville, only about a two-hour drive from her own hometown. But apart from being black, the two had little in common. Even if they had, the roommate said little and went home every weekend. Ironically, Kitty realized that she was actually more comfortable with the white students in the women's dorm. As it happened, staying in the dorm for hours at a time, especially during curfew, and listening to the other girls' chatter forced her to interact with them and they with her. She began to hear their stories and to understand who they were and how they moved through the world.

Kitty did well in her first-year classes and made some good friends. She took a writing class and found her niche. *I can do this*, she told herself. *I can really do this.*

And then, as spring came around, she joined several of the other students in becoming a "big sister," a sophomore mentor to connect with and guide an incoming freshman. She wrote to her little sister over the summer and found herself looking forward to meeting her in person.

The first day of the fall semester, she spotted the young girl by her nametag at freshman orientation. She was vivacious and blond, with blue eyes, a little upturned nose and pale skin. Kitty approached her and introduced herself and gave her all the information she could think of to help acclimate her. The two began to talk regularly. Kitty invited her little sister to dinner, but she said she couldn't make it, and Kitty didn't ask again.

One day, the roommate offered to teach Kitty how to shave her legs.

"Why would I want to do that?" she asked.

"Why? Shaved legs are so much nicer on a girl. All the guys think so, anyway."

Kitty grinned. "Not in my community. I wish I had some hair on my legs. It's considered attractive."

"For real?" The girl's eyes opened very wide, as if she'd just been told that Kitty was from Mars. "What a relief that must be for you!"

"Are you kidding? It's easier to shave legs than to grow hair that doesn't exist!"

When another student on the floor pushed in the restroom door, she was surprised to find the two young women doubled over with laughter.

Kitty saw her little sister through her first year's academic struggles, boyfriends and parties. One night, they were painting their nails, laughing and talking. Then a companionable silence fell between them.

All at once, the young girl said, "Look, I have to tell you something." Her face, Kitty noticed, was paler than usual, and her mouth set in a straight line.

"When I met you," she began slowly, "when I got to campus and saw that you were my big sister, I couldn't believe it. Truly, I felt sick. I didn't know any col—Negro girls, and I was just so put off. I actually called my folks and said, 'Why me? Why would I get her?'

"Then you invited me out to dinner," the girl continued. I didn't have anything else to do—I just didn't want to go. I was so embarrassed to be seen with you."

Kitty felt her shoulders tense. She wasn't as surprised that this would be someone's reaction at the university as that it would be *this* girl's reaction, her new friend. She thought her radar was good for things like this. She thought she could smell prejudice a mile away, but she hadn't received any signals.

"I just wanted to tell you that," the girl said. "But I don't feel any of that anymore. Now that I've gotten to know you, I'd go anywhere with you. Really and truly. I'd be proud to be seen with you, Kitty."

Kitty remained close with her little sister; she even invited her to her wedding. How could she blame her for telling the truth about the racial divide the nation has continued to struggle with for so long? But she never got over the fact that she had not only witnessed but actually caused such a profound change in someone—just by being who she was. That was an education in itself.

7
FAKAHATCHEE ARCHAEOLOGY

I think this story is one of the most important in the book, and it was one of the most difficult to write. It serves as an important barometer of how times, and attitudes, have changed—in Florida and elsewhere. There was a period, as we know, when locals saw the unique ecosystem that is the Florida Everglades as so much swampland that needed to be drained and developed in order to become useful. There also was a time when people dug up ancient human skulls without thinking of anything but a trophy. And there was a time when the ethics of unearthing a sacred burial mound would not have occurred to the average hunter.

Fakahatchee Strand, where much of the story is set, is a one-hundred-square-mile patch of swamp forest located in Big Cypress, a part of the Everglades about two and a half hours northwest of Miami. Known as the orchid and bromeliad capital of North America, it is also home to bald cypress and royal palms, endangered Florida panthers and black bears, Everglades minks and diamondback terrapins, and an astonishing array of bird life, such as the roseate spoonbill and bald eagle. In addition to providing habitats for endangered and rare plants and animals, the wetlands are also important to humans because it filters water and helps prevent flooding.

I meet octogenarian Eddie Rennolds in advance of a storytelling performance I was doing on behalf of Florida Humanities in LaBelle. LaBelle is the county seat of Hendry Couny, south of the Caloosahatchee River. My host, Joe Thomas, the guiding light of the LaBelle Heritage Museum, had recommended Mr. Rennolds to me as an excellent source for

"I'm Really Proud of You, Dad": People and Places

It used to be common to collect human skulls as artifacts. *Eugene_w, freeimages.com.*

a local story, as Eddie had lived in LaBelle all his life. In fact, I had heard the end of this story—Joe's portion—before I recorded the beginning.

As we sat outside the main room where the show was to take place, I found Eddie to be a wonderful storyteller: friendly, generous and knowledgeable. Dressed as he was in a hunting cap and jacket, I could easily visualize his tale. I particularly liked his use of the descriptive name *Thickahatchee* for the area.

THE YEAR WAS 1974, and Eddie Rennolds was enjoying one of his favorite activities, hunting. That day he had taken his dog to the Fakahatchee, as he often did. His blue tick was running a deer, but he couldn't see very far ahead because of the denseness of the foliage. (Hence the nickname *Thickahatchee*.) To increase the visibility, he crouched down on the ground. First, he saw the deer, and then he saw the dog following it. And then, raising his eyes a bit, he saw something else. At first, he thought he was experiencing a vision. But there it was, a good-sized Indian mound.

Eddie scrambled to his feet and made his way through the trees to the mound. He figured it was about two hundred feet wide and maybe forty feet high. Slowly, he circled the perimeter. It looked to him as though nobody had touched it before. He couldn't attend to it then, so he took off his white T-shirt, tore it into several long strips and flagged the way out of there so he could return to the site later on.

He thought about that mound for the rest of the week. He had been digging around for bones since he was a child, but he had found only living mounds, with beads or the kind of animal bones that the Natives must have thrown out after finishing a meal. Was this that same kind of shallow living mound, the kind filled with a layer of animal bones, then a layer of sand to prevent the flies, then another layer of animal bones? There was one just west of LaBelle, about a mile from the bridge, and another up the river a mile. By now, the dredge had covered them up with fill, so they were no good to anyone anymore. Was this one of those, or could it be a deeper burial mound, with human skeletons? He couldn't wait to find out.

That weekend, he drove back to the Fakahatchee and made camp in his usual spot. Then he followed the strips of cloth back to the site, this time without the dog. He saw a small ditch he hadn't noticed the first time, but he was too curious about the mound to pay attention. With the shovel he'd brought, he started clearing away the dirt. He unearthed one foot of dirt from the single hole and held his breath. Nothing. That meant it was much deeper, which signaled that it was a burial ground. It took quite a bit more digging until he found five skulls, arranged in a star-like pattern. A little more work revealed that the skulls belonged to five skeletons, buried standing up. He couldn't believe what he had found. It was almost better than treasure. In fact, it *was* treasure.

It was getting late, and Eddie decided to head back to camp. He chose one of the skulls to take with him as a souvenir. As he made his way through the brush, however, his ankle caught in a thick vine, and he tripped. He was fine, but the skull fell to the ground. He righted himself and bent down to pick it up, but it had shattered. All he had left was the top of the skull and the jawbone.

Eddie had left the trail markers in place, and not long afterward he returned to the spot a third time. This time, he fixed his attention on the ditch that he hadn't seen the first day. It was fairly narrow, with flat rocks—smaller pieces of what was all around—stacked up along the sides. He followed the ditch down nearly a mile to a place called Calloway Slough, which runs south from Immokalee to the Gulf of Mexico. It seems that someone had dug a canal right to the mound. There was a gumbo limbo tree about eighteen inches in diameter, which meant it had been at that spot a good long time, he knew, because the species grows so slowly.

I have to come back here with a metal detector, he thought. *See what else is buried.* But he never did. Instead, he returned to the mound and gathered all the bones from the five people buried there. He climbed the gumbo limbo and carved his initials into its bark. Then he took those bones with him back to town.

What do you do with ancient bones? His first thought was to take them home and glue them back together, but by the time he got them back to camp, they were already too broken up. He thought about those bones all night. In the morning, he knew what he had to do. He took the sack over to Art and Kari Rice at the LaBelle Heritage Museum. The museum already possessed many artifacts he and others had found around the area, including bones from eohippus (the ancestor of the modern horse), mastodon and giant sloth. It seemed like the perfect place.

The Rices welcomed Eddie to the small museum and eagerly took a look at the bones. They contacted a local professor of archaeology, and Eddie showed him where he had found them. It was determined that the remains might have been skeletons of Native peoples or they might have belonged to settlers. There was no real way of knowing, in part because the bones had been buried in rock that could have moved when the nearby Caloosahatchee River was dredged.

For thirty years, the museum kept the bones in a glass-topped display case for people to look at and learn from. It never received a single complaint. Then, one day, a professor from Edison State College in Fort Myers suggested that the museum was "skating on thin ice" by displaying the bones, and the curators should send them to a Native American organization opposed to the exploitation of ancestral remains. Joe Thomas, who was museum president at the time, arranged to send the skeletons, with a letter of explanation, back where they came from. Back home to the earth.

8
A MAR-A-LAGO MEMORY

1100 South Ocean Boulevard isn't quite as famous an American address as 1600 Pennsylvania Avenue, but it's going down in the annals of presidential history just the same. That's the address of Mar-a-Lago, built between 1924 and 1927 for cereal heiress Marjorie Merriweather Post, and most recently acquired by President Donald Trump. A National Historic Landmark, Mar-a-Lago is a 128-room resort occupying more than sixty thousand square feet of Palm Beach—not including the golf club.

This story takes place at the mansion, but its heroes come from elsewhere: G-Star School of the Arts for Film, Animation and Performing Arts, a top-performing public charter high school located in Palm Springs, just five miles—and perhaps a few hundred million dollars—southwest. The alumnus who gave me this story had long since matriculated as a student at Florida Atlantic University. But he was still just a bit starry-eyed when he recounted it.

It's worth adding a word about the school's X-Scream program, founded in 2005. Not only has the X-Scream team developed and run the third-largest haunted house in Florida, but it also produces dinner theater, flash mob and dance performances and engages in disaster drills with members of Fire Rescue, the FBI, Homeland Security and more. It's community engagement at its finest, as well as most dramatic.

And speaking of community engagement, this experience occurred years before the property was ever used as "White House South."

"I'm Really Proud of You, Dad": People and Places

Mar-a-Lago was built by Marjorie Merriweather Post in the 1920s. *State Archives of Florida.*

BY HIS SENIOR YEAR of high school, Joey DeCelles had participated in four years of X-Scream extravaganzas. That year, the theme for the haunted house was Old London. Think Jack the Ripper Old London, as in prostitutes, drunks, beggars and bobbies in old-fashioned police uniforms. Joey played a bobby. At the close of another successful Halloween season, the team hung up its costumes with the thought that someday they might be needed again.

That day came just as the year was drawing to a close. By late November and early December, the team was hitting the books, anticipating a restful, or at least playful, Christmas break, once those pesky exams were over.

Then they got an offer that was too good to refuse. Their director assembled the group for the announcement.

"Anyone who worked the Haunt who wants to use those costumes and characters again, I've got something for you," the director said. "I need volunteers for a Salvation Army charity event. It's just about five miles from here. We can all take a van."

"Where is it?" somebody asked.

"Mar-a-Lago. In Palm Beach."

He waited while the undercurrent of murmurs wore itself out. Then he said, "Actually, it's pretty sweet. You'll each get paid fifty dollars." He offered a few more details, such as date, starting and ending times.

"So what exactly do we have to do there?" Joey asked.

"What you did at the haunted house, basically. Improv. So," the man said, clapping his hands. "What do you say? I could really use you."

Ten of the students signed up, and one of them was Joey.

"So I had this idea," the director continued. "I was thinking that instead of just being the drunks, beggars and so forth that you were before, we dress one of you"—here he looked at the smallest of the students—"as an elf on the shelf."

"What's an elf on the shelf?" This from one of the foreign students.

"It's a Christmas tradition. One of Santa's little elves watches each child to be sure they're naughty or nice. Then they report back to Santa, and he decides whether to give them a gift. But they're really little. Hence the shelf."

The girl nodded.

"So anyway, this elf can run around, causing mischief, hiding, doing stuff like that. And the rest of you can riff on that. Ask people if they've seen him. Complain about him. Try to catch him. Try to involve them. Get the picture?"

The students looked at each other, not at all convinced. But fifty dollars was more than they'd see in quite a while. They figured they'd figure it out.

"Sure," Joey said. "Why not?"

The day of the gig was a long one. The students attended their classes and then changed into their costumes, hopped into the van and made the short drive to the mansion. It was so different there, however, that they might as well have gone to Tasmania.

"I'm Really Proud of You, Dad": People and Places

"Oh my God!" someone sang out as they turned down the drive. "I can't believe how big it is!"

"It's amazing!"

"Does one person really own this place?" Joey asked. "This is one person's property, all of this?"

No one said anything in response. The van turned past the golf course and into the parking lot. As they clambered out, the students heard soft music. Meanwhile, their director gave them the rundown. How to behave. Dos and don'ts. Nothing surprising.

They turned a corner, and an officious-looking young woman with a clipboard came forward to greet them. She gave them the same information that the director had and then led them to the back of the building. They saw two enormous staircases wrapped around the ornate exterior. And then they stopped, all ten of them, plus the director, their eyes nearly popping out of their heads. There in front of them was a magnificent outdoor pool.

"Like something out of *The Great Gatsby*!" Joey gasped. And that's when the nerves hit him. Because around that fancy pool were the most gorgeous people he had ever seen, dressed in shimming black gowns, with strands of pearls and diamonds and stiletto heels or in black tie with shiny shoes. The hairstyles alone must have cost a fortune, he reflected. What's a bunch of high schoolers doing here?

Their job, actually. And that's what they did. They began to improvise, all the time painfully aware that they hadn't played their characters for about a month and a half. But they were theater kids, and, as they say, the show must go on.

At first, they tried to mingle with the well-heeled guests. But for fifteen or twenty minutes they found it impossible to connect with anyone. Whether it was that the people were not interested, or they were too interested in their tight groups, or whatever it was, the kids cracked jokes and asked if anyone had seen the elf on the shelf, and no one gave them the time of day. The food runners passed with champagne and caviar like something out of a movie—exactly, Joey reflected, like what you'd expect at a Mar-a-Lago party. Meanwhile, the minutes ticked by, and nothing, improv-wise, was clicking.

They all met up in a corner of the pool area to regroup.

"What do you think?" the elf said. "We're bombing. This is the pits."

"It's really uncomfortable," one of the young women said, nodding.

"They hate us. They want to talk to their friends. So would I."

"Tell you what," someone said. "Why don't we stop trying to interact? Let's just do our business next to them."

So they tried that. Having heated conversations about the elf. Trying to flush him out of a hedge. Laughing at his antics. And it worked. Heads began to turn toward them. People made obvious attempts to overhear their conversations.

The elf began to loosen up. He picked up glasses of champagne left on tables and sipped them. And suddenly, it seemed as though everyone wanted in on the fun. It was no longer intimidating for the students. It was a game they were all playing, every one of them. And Joey felt the weight of fear rush off him like water. *I'm not going to see any of these people ever again*, he realized. *Let's just make our silly impression on these $500-a-plate fat cats.*

They were having such a great time they didn't notice at first that those fat cats were slowly being ushered inside for the real entertainment. Their director approached them, followed closely by the woman who had met them in the parking lot.

"You guys were fabulous!" she said, grinning and shaking her head.

"You really knocked it out of the park," their director added. "I was watching everything. I'm so proud of you!"

"Wait right here," the woman said. She opened a massive wooden door, and the students caught a glimpse of—was someone actually swinging from the ceiling?

"We were the opening act for *that*?" The elf whistled. "Wow!"

When the woman returned, she handed an envelope to the director. "Here's the checks for you all," she said. "And here is a little something special." She proceeded to give each of them a small gift bag.

"Did you just throw this together for us?" Joey asked. "That's so nice of you!"

"No, these are the goodie bags for the guests. We had some extras, and because you did so well, we wanted you to have them." She smiled at each student. Then she looked at the director. "I've really got to go back in now," she said. "Thanks again! You were awesome!"

Back in the van, the students checked out their gift bags with the help of the light from their cellphones. They held Christmas ornaments made from Swarovski crystal and tiny bags of exquisite chocolates. When Joey reached home, he immediately looked up the price of the ornaments online. They were worth one hundred dollars apiece. That plus the fifty-dollar checks wasn't bad for an evening's work for high school students.

But it was perfectly appropriate for actors who had played their roles with such style.

9
HELP WANTED
Must Farm

Care to sample some delicious ackee and salt fish, staples of the Jamaican national cuisine? Look no further than Florida. Not only are Jamaicans the largest group of Caribbean immigrants in the United States but also about a quarter million, one out of every four, are here. That's second only to New York. What's more, most Jamaican Floridians reside in South Florida. And although Kendall is one of the original Jamaican enclaves in Miami-Dade County, Lauderhill, in west Broward, has been dubbed "Jamaica Hill" due to its wealth of Jamaican residents and elected officials.

While political and economic upheaval were behind the most recent immigration wave that began in the 1970s, the "Jamerican" saga is actually much older. In fact, the Jamaican/U.S. immigration story began with the islanders' assisting this country rather than the other way around. In 1619, twenty Jamaican and other Caribbean islanders with "free person" status volunteered to come over on a Dutch frigate as indentured workers in the famous Jamestown, Virginia settlement.

A much larger wave of Jamaican immigration occurred in the early part of the twentieth century. After that, Americans began to invite Jamaicans as "swallow migrants" to help with the harvest on a temporary basis. Then, during World War II, farm labor shortages due to the draft received special federal attention. Congress enacted laws that allowed Caribbean workers once again to fill much-needed roles in the fields—and 75,000 Jamaicans and Bahamians answered the call to work on farms throughout Florida.

Jamaicans and Bahamians were invited to Florida in order to farm sugar cane. *State Archives of Florida*.

In fact, between 1930 and 1940 alone, the population of Belle Glade, where much of this story is set, more than tripled from under 1,000 to more than 3,800.

This is where Tanya Wilson's Florida story begins, about seventy-five years ago, with her grandfather Papa David. I met Tanya at a Palm Beach County Planning Commission event, where I was scheduled to speak about the importance of storytelling in building community. As you will see, she understands that message loud and clear.

IN THE EARLY 1940s, David Clarke was living the life he had always envisioned for himself growing up in St. James, Jamaica. A successful farmer in the parish of Manchester, he owned over forty acres of farmland on which he raised sugarcane and a few varieties of citrus. His business supported several workers, both permanent and temporary. His family was well fed; his children were in school. He had a fine reputation among his

"I'm Really Proud of You, Dad": People and Places

neighbors. Of course, if he had had a little more money he could have expanded, but he had plenty of patience.

And then one late summer evening after supper, Clarke was scanning the paper when an ad caught his eye. Due to the advent of war, the U.S. government had instituted a special farm workers' program that circumvented immigration quotas. Farmers were needed, and the pay was good.

David didn't have to think very long. He looked over at his wife, who was leaning over her sewing. He knew it would be hard on her if he left for a while. But she was capable. They had raised their two children to take responsibility. And the extra cash could change their lives.

"So Agnes, what would you say if I went to America for a while?" he asked. "Says here they're looking for farmers. I could make enough American dollars to set us up for life. What do you say?"

His wife looked up and gave him a sly grin. "I'd say you're going to do it whatever I say. Just don't like it so much you don't come back to us."

"I won't stay long; I promise. A year maybe. That's all. The time will pass before you know it."

Soon after that conversation, David Clarke kissed his wife, son and daughter good-bye and, along with a good number of his fellow farmers, boarded a ship bound for the States. A cruise liner, it wasn't. The voyage was like nothing he had ever imagined. His living space was tiny and airless, and the waves pitched the ship around the sea like a child playing with a toy duck in the bath. All he could think was: Look how I, a free man, am making my way to America! Like little better than cargo! Only my enslaved African ancestors could have had a worse trip going to the New World!

Then, just when David thought the voyage couldn't get more uncomfortable, the war intervened. At the time, travel in the waters around Florida was fraught with danger. German U-boats targeted—and sank—dozens of American ships. Throughout the journey, therefore, a U.S. fighter jet served as an armed guard overhead. It was reassuring, but it was also terrifying.

Arriving in Miami at last, David Clarke and his fellow travelers each received a dog tag with a tracking number that enabled them to work as migratory government laborers. Then they made the eighty-five-mile ride to Belle Glade, on the southeast shore of Lake Okeechobee. At first glance, it certainly bore no small resemblance to home. He and his fellow workers were enthusiastic about the opportunity to make money and experience a new country. Those early few weeks they approached their work with gusto and often joked about the improvements they'd make on their farms back in Jamaica with their American dollars.

But then winter set in, and with it came a bone-rattling cold that the Caribbean farmers had never experienced. To make matters worse, they lived in makeshift shelters that were a far cry from the comfortable homes they had left behind. And while a certain camaraderie developed among the farmers, they mainly spent their all-too-little free time complaining to one another. About the poor treatment they received from the overseers. About how much they missed their families. And about something else they had rarely experienced back home: racism. Being called "boy" by people younger than they were. Being spat at. And worse.

"I know I'm not a landowner here," Clarke would tell anyone who would listen. "But I'm not a child or an animal either. They invited me to come; I didn't ask for this. The least they could do is treat me with a little respect."

The man in the next bunk laughed. "Respect? For us? Where do you think you are?"

The seasons changed, and still David toiled in the cane fields. He picked citrus and various winter vegetables and prepared them for market. It was not unfamiliar labor, and it wasn't even the hardest work he had ever done. But he missed his old life. And then one day, he had simply had enough. He couldn't put his finger on what had tipped the scales for him. But after just six months, he returned to Miami and boarded the ship that took him back to his family, his farm and his country.

When Agnes welcomed her husband back home, she whispered into his ear four words: "Was it worth it?"

He didn't hesitate for an instant. "Sure. It was the right thing to do. But coming home feels more right."

David Clarke never renewed his American government migrant labor contract. He never returned to the United States, either. But nearly forty years later, in 1978, his daughter Lolethia, born in Kingston, made the trip from Jamaica to Miami like her father before her—this time by plane. Like him, she responded to a call for workers. A registered nurse back home, she was recruited by Mercy Hospital to work in an intensive care unit. She stayed for only a few years before returning home, just as her father had done.

Then, in 1993, Jackson Memorial Hospital recruited her, and she returned to Miami. This time, her sixteen-year-old daughter, Tanya, came to the States too, to study at Broward Community College in the Fort Lauderdale area. Now an urban planner in North Miami, Tanya looks back at her grandfather's saga and feels nothing but pride in her own special kind of American family and its contributions to the country that invited it here.

10

A BIBLIOTHÈQUE IN MIAMI GARDENS

According to the 2010 Census, Florida was home to more than 375,000 Haitian Americans, more than any other state in the nation. Every year, the Haitian community increases here, and so does its voice. In fact, Palm Beach, Broward and Miami-Dade Counties have all elected officials from the Caribbean island.

Here's another surprising statistic: The National Center on Children in Poverty reported that in 2016, 36 percent of African American and Afro-Caribbean children in the Sunshine State lived in poverty—well above both the state and national rates—at a time when Florida had the fourth-largest economy in the nation.

The following tale brings faces and names to these factoids. I have known Lucrèce Louisdhon-Louinis, first as a colleague, then as a friend, for over a decade. A former librarian and library administrator, she currently directs the Louines Louinis Haitian Dance Theater Inc. When I asked her for a story to showcase the Haitian American experience in Florida, she didn't hesitate. This isn't the only immigrant success story in this book, but it is perhaps the only one that portrays how an entire community benefited from a team led by a newcomer who instantly knew her place: here.

ON THE FIRST DAY of her new job, Lucrèce Louisdhon-Louinis walked into the dark, sad-looking children's department at the Miami Gardens branch library and almost cried. It was the late nineties, and she had just left a

Only in Florida

Lucrèce Louisdhon-Louinis performs in traditional Haitian clothing. *Courtesy of Lucrèce Louisdhon-Louinis.*

library position she loved in Queens, New York, in order to care for her ailing mother. She had relocated to Florida with her three-year-old son; her husband would join them the following year. So for the next few months, it would be just her, her mother, her child—and this.

Lucrèce had known she would work with books since she'd first arrived in this country in 1980. Having grown up in the bookstore owned by her father, Ludovic Louisdhon, back home, she went to New York as a foreign student to learn how to pursue their shared dream: turning the family business into the largest bookstore and publishing house in Haiti. She fully expected to finish her degree and return home.

When she applied for college, however, her English was poor. She had seen the word *library* in the catalogue and thought that was her major, because in French, a *librairie* is a bookstore. Instead, she found herself in library science courses for work in a *bibliothèque*, the French word for library. When she explained to her father her mistake, he told her not to worry.

"You're not upset, Papi?" she asked him.

"Of course not! You'll still be working with books. The only difference is that now you can give them out for free!"

What is it about making plans? Lucrèce specialized in children's library resources. After graduation, she was ready to pursue her life's work in Haiti, but by then, the political system in her home country had drastically deteriorated.

"There's nothing for you here anymore," her father told her. "It's not a good place to open such a large business. Your home is in the States now."

"I'm Really Proud of You, Dad": People and Places

She set about making the best of her situation, finding work at a library in Broward County. Children's librarians tell stories, and little by little, because of the local Haitian population, she found her voice as a teller of Haitian folktales. In that capacity, she visited libraries all over the area and discovered that both the families and her fellow librarians responded enthusiastically to her performances of the folktales she had learned as a child. She started to make a name for herself. *How ironic*, she thought. *Discovering my Haitian cultural roots here in the United States.*

But that was then. Now here she was, in a low-income neighborhood in Miami Gardens, watching the children of African American and Afro-Caribbean families on the ratty furnishings and frayed rug under time-worn posters and dim lights. There were no special programs for them as far as she could tell. To her eyes, there was no fun at all.

By now, she knew it wasn't like this at every library in the area. But this was the closest branch to her new home that had posted an opening in a children's department. She sighed. With visions of the colorful, dynamic program she had left in New York lingering in her head, she was expected to manage a department that put her in mind of Dickens. Charles Dickens. Think *Oliver Twist*. "Please, sir. I want some more."

Some people might have sweated it out, happy to have found a job in their field within a reasonable commute from the house. And some people would have said, "Well, I'm new here. Let me take some time to get acquainted with the people and the place." But not Lucrèce. After spending a single day in that depressing place, she began to dream up ways to improve it.

Then she requested a meeting with her boss, who closed her office door and returned to her desk before responding to her suggestions.

"Who do you think you are?" the older woman hissed. "You're telling me I don't know how to run a library?"

"Of course not," replied Lucrèce, crossing her fingers under the table. "It's just that we could bring a happier feel to the place. We could be more open and inviting. Offer entertaining programs to these kids. You know they don't have much at home. Some of them are really struggling. They deserve better."

"You think I don't know what these children deserve?" the woman growled, rising to her feet. "Well, let me tell you a thing or two. First of all, I know this neighborhood; these are my people. Second, what makes you think that just because you're some kind of storytelling celebrity from New York, you can do whatever you want? That doesn't count for anything around here. I am not going to do what *you* want."

And so Lucrèce did it herself. She talked to the Friends of the Library, the volunteer community group that supports library programming with time, money and other resources. She asked them to help her pay to bring in storytellers. Then she made friends with the head maintenance man of the library, speaking to him in French and calling him *cher*, or "darling." Somehow, he came up with the nicer, brighter furniture they needed. He also improved the lighting.

Soon it was almost Kwanzaa, the African winter celebration, and Lucrèce decided to put on a special event for the children. She asked the staff to help her decorate the low tables in the department with Kwanzaa symbols and dress up for the occasion in colorful African garb. Lucrèce's newly arrived husband, Louines, a veteran performer, agreed to bring his drums.

The morning of the event, Lucrèce paced up and down the children's department, checking on every detail. Her husband arrived, bringing her little son in tow. And when the other children appeared, and the drumming started, and the storyteller began, she could see it in everyone's eyes: parents and staff included. This was what this community needed. A celebration of itself.

After everyone had left, one of the staff members took her aside.

"Congratulations," she said, giving her a hug. "It was great."

"We all did it together," Lucrèce replied.

"Yes, but it was your idea. And I've got to tell you—when you started here, we were taking bets on how long you would last."

The rest is, literally, Miami-Dade Library System history. Lucrèce stayed in the Miami Gardens branch long enough to receive the grudging acceptance of her boss. Then she applied for a job as the assistant children's coordinator for the system, which she had done in New York. Here, the position required mainly programming skills. And Lucrèce knew programming. She took a small, disrespected storytelling initiative and, with the help of the main system storyteller, turned it into an international exchange festival, with librarians and tellers traveling back and forth to countries such as France, Ghana, Argentina—and, of course, Haiti. The wildly successful festival lasted thirteen years, with the final one taking place the year after she moved on and formed her own company with her husband.

In 2016, Lucrèce and Louines shared the prestigious Florida Folk Heritage Award for their work on behalf of African American and Afro-Caribbean culture. All for doing what came naturally: honoring a community's heritage.

11
HOW MUCH IS ENOUGH?

When it comes to the opioid epidemic, Florida has it all: so-called pill mills where doctors prescribe painkillers for locals and tourists who've heard about the lax regulations—and hundreds of substance abuse rehab centers to deal with the problems they create. It's not that we can boast of the most opioid-related deaths; as of 2017, we lost that distinction to Ohio. But in the past decade, ninety of the most prolific one hundred opioid prescribers in the country hung out their shingles in the Sunshine State. In fact, in 2010, approximately *half a billion* of the little pills were sold here.

It should come as no surprise that Florida plays host to such prodigious substance abuse. The 1980s hit TV show *Miami Vice* couldn't have survived without the cocaine boom, and decades earlier, Al Capone made a pretty penny off of illegal alcohol here during the Prohibition era. You might say this newest scourge is simply Party Favor 3.0.

Not that cocaine is exactly yesterday's news. In September 2019, a couple made an interesting find on a Florida beach: a $30,000 brick of cocaine washed up by the latest hurricane. That same week, another beachgoer turned in a duffel bag with fifteen bricks of the stuff.

Speaking of parties, I met Shirlee and Steve Hammond (name changed to protect their professional anonymity) at a holiday party not long before their marriage. I was immediately taken first by their differences—she is blond, curly-haired and adorable, and he is, well, 6'4"—and also by the fact that they are both gregarious and high-spirited. As private investigators in the Fort Myers area, the couple sometimes find themselves tackling the opioid issue

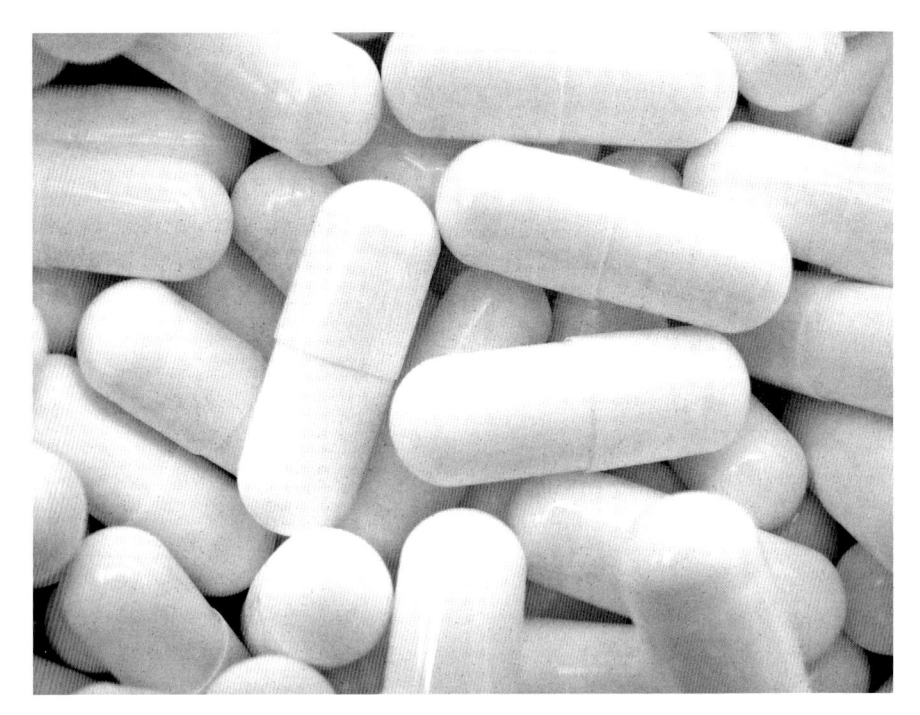

When it comes to the opioid epidemic, Florida has it all. *Marcin Jochimczyk, freeimages.com*.

head on and occasionally without even expecting to. This story highlights just how pervasive the drug crisis is and how surprising are some of the players.

It started off as a simple custody battle. The ex-husband of a successful doctor claimed that he deserved to raise his children because she had taken them out of state against the divorce court's express orders. But that wasn't the half of it. She was also behaving grossly inappropriately with them. And he suspected that she was somehow involved with selling drugs and hiding her ill-gotten gains in offshore accounts.

Shirlee and Steve, who had been referred by a friend, figured it was a two-person job. Shirlee had worked as a private investigator for more than thirty years, the last few of them there in Fort Myers, and her husband was a retired cop who had been a PI for well over a decade. They were a good team. Needless to say, as a couple, they had each other's backs. But it was more than that. After seven years of marriage, they knew each other's thoughts and could anticipate each other's actions. You might call them a well-oiled investigating machine.

"I'm Really Proud of You, Dad": People and Places

The two immediately set to work gathering intel. There are all sorts of ways to do this, of course. Surveillance. Going through court and public records. Or Shirlee's personal favorite: using some pretext to gain a person's trust, such as stopping someone to ask for directions and then getting into a different conversation altogether.

In this case, they made several visits to the doctor's offices when they knew she wasn't around, asking people who worked nearby about her, making up stories to gather information. They also watched her. And what they learned shocked Shirlee for one of the few times in her long and eventful career.

They discovered that the doctor owned a stately home in a classy neighborhood, expensive late-model cars and, in general, an extraordinarily elegant lifestyle. But what their research didn't tell them, Shirlee—dressed in medical scrubs as a cover—learned when the two women shared an elevator in the doctor's fancy office building. The doctor was in her forties and, to put it mildly, a knockout. She looked for all the world like a perfectly polished, highly respectable physician. Or maybe more like a movie star playing one. *What was someone like her doing mixed up in all of this?* Shirlee wondered.

The next evening, after everyone but the cleaners had supposedly gone home, she and Steve parked their car some distance from the medical building—only on television does the surveillance car sit across the street from the target—and started filming. One by one, a series of emaciated, ill-looking men, most of them slack-jawed and ragged, approached the door, hit a button on the intercom system, said something into the speaker and were buzzed in. The two PIs filmed them coming into the building empty-handed and emerging several minutes later with small packages.

After about six people performed the ritual, Shirlee said, "I'm going in." She left the car, walked slowly to the building and stood behind the man at the intercom, listening to what he was saying. As she did, another man walked out.

"Hey," she said, as casually as she could. "Did you just go up to see Dr. ____?"

The young man nodded, albeit reluctantly.

"I'm trying to get up there, but I can't get through now. I saw her last week; I can't understand it." He just stared.

"You got some oxy, right?" she continued. "What else does she have? Does she have fentanyl too? She's got good stuff, doesn't she?"

His eyes narrowed a little. "You say you know her?"

"Yeah, man. Don't sweat it. I'll get in somehow. See you later, man."

When she returned to the car, it was Steve's turn. He had dressed for the occasion in a ripped T-shirt and dirty jeans, with rubber flip-flops on his unwashed feet. Looking as he did like one of the customers, he was able to get the exact names of the products from a few of them. Then the two PIs returned to the office and ran the tags of the cars in the parking lot through the computer. It was obvious that several of the visitors had drug problems; they had arrest records to prove it.

The following day, the two presented their evidence to the contact, who passed it along to the ex-husband. It was only a matter of time before the whole thing ended up in court, although the custody charges were adjudicated separately from the drug charges.

"Can you identify the woman you were tailing?" Shirlee was asked on the witness stand.

"Of course." She pointed. "She's that beautiful young woman sitting over there, in the cream-colored blouse."

When the two had finished testifying, Shirlee and Steve walked out of the building and stood for a moment around the corner. It wasn't long before the doctor and her new boyfriend, a well-dressed businessman, came outside and began a loud argument. Needless to say, they didn't know they were being eavesdropped on by professionals.

"I told you not to come in that car!" he screamed. "Don't you think such a nice ride shows we've got cash? You never listen to me!"

The couple eventually walked to their car in silence. As they pulled away, Shirlee said, "You know, when they asked me to identify the perpetrator, I said, 'She's that beautiful young woman sitting over there, in the cream-colored blouse.'"

Steve, who had testified after her, looked over in surprise. "I can't believe it! I said the exact same thing!"

Shirlee sighed. "I know after all this time I shouldn't let these things get to me. But I can't help it. Sometimes I take these cases personally."

"I know." Her husband nodded. "This one was really hard."

"I mean, why risk everything like that? How hard she must have had to work to get to where she was? She'll never practice medicine again. And her kids? What is worth losing your kids?"

"Men do it all the time," he said quietly.

"Yeah. But we women should know better. We should know when enough is enough."

To no one's surprise, the doctor was found guilty and sent to prison—all for selling pills for maybe fifty dollars apiece. Cash only, of course. Isn't it always about the cash?

12
GOLF, OF COURSE

According to dailycommercial.com, Florida is home to more than one thousand golf courses—more than any other state. At about 8 percent of the nation's total, that's what you might call a whole lot of green. Sadly, for lovers of the sport, developers have started seeing opportunities for another kind of green elsewhere, and the diminishing number of golf courses reflects that changing financial incentive. In fact, the National Golf Foundation in Jupiter (Florida) noted the state lost more than four hundred courses in the last few years. It seems that fewer young people are, um, getting into the swing.

Nevertheless, when we think Sunshine State, we still tend to think golf. Not that the sport began here, not by a long shot. Historians locate its origins in Scotland in the fifteenth century.

Many of those who love the sport today—professionals and amateurs alike—date their obsession, like Peter Wegmann, to their childhoods. And that makes this story all the more poignant, because golf is not just a young man's game, especially not in Florida. Senior championships and age fifty-five-plus golf club communities abound, with people who used to carry their own clubs now briskly traversing the course on electric carts. Well into their nineties.

FLORIDA REALTOR PETER WEGMANN has been playing golf for close to sixty years—and he's only sixty-two. He grew up in Plantation, next door to U.S.

Florida has the most golf courses of any state in the United States. *freeimages.com*.

Open champ Julius Boros, who, according to the World Golf Hall of Fame, was known for his "effortless ease, flawless technique, and hidden competitive fire." Boros was PGA Player of the Year in 1952 and 1956 and led the earnings list in 1952 and 1955. Most importantly for our story, perhaps, at age forty-three Boros was the oldest winner of the U.S. Open since Ted Ray won at the same age more than forty years earlier.

Peter started playing golf because the champ, who had become a pro, started his kids on the sport at a young age. Growing up in Florida, of course, he could play all year long, and he got quite good at the game. In amateur golf circles, the age of a "senior" can be as young as forty-five. Over the years, he's played in amateur golf championships all over the world, including the Canadian Men's Senior Amateur Championship, the British Senior Amateur and the U.S. Golf Association Senior Amateur. He even won the Florida State Golf Association Senior Amateur and Senior Match Play in the same year. Any way you slice it, that's a lot of golf.

A couple of years back, Peter Wegmann found himself playing at the ultra-exclusive Founders Club in Sarasota-Bradenton, which advertises itself as "700 acres of lakes, fairways and nature preserves," with just over 260 homes and a course designed by the legendary golf course architect Robert Trent Jones Jr.

"I'm Really Proud of You, Dad": People and Places

This particular day, Peter was taking part in the Florida State Golf Association Senior Match Play. Match play means that each golfer (or team) plays against one opponent only and gains a point for each hole he or she wins. That day, eighty-six people played thirty-six holes to qualify; then the best thirty-two golfers were seeded according to their scores. First place played thirty-second place, number two played thirty-one, and so on, in brackets. When a golfer won four matches, the player advanced to the finals.

At one point in the match, Peter was in a bracket against a man named Jerry, whom he had met before and knew to be a snowbird, a winter resident, from Minnesota. They had played a practice round at the Florida State Senior Amateur on another course in Ocala, Florida, in 2016, and Peter had gone on to win. That was the only other time he had seen the man.

Peter and Jerry had advanced to the finals, and they were at about the sixth or seventh hole when Peter noticed a strange thing. In fact, in his experience, it was downright bizarre. Normally, no one but the marshals and the scorekeeper watched what the golfers were doing in these championships. After all, this wasn't Tiger Woods; these were senior amateurs. They didn't expect TV cameras. They didn't even expect their wives and children. An audience was unheard of.

But there, undeniably, was a small crowd. Admittedly, a very small crowd. But no fewer than five or six golf carts filled with seniors had gathered a respectful distance away. Was this possibly for him, Peter wondered, with no small amount of pride. He had a few wins under his belt, after all. And he'd played an awful lot in the state over the years. Had his reputation preceded him? Could it be?

Then he heard the cheers. "Je-rry! Je-rrry!" Older men, dressed in the loose-fitting whites and pastels of Floridians of a certain class and age, were on their feet now, supporting his opponent with all their lungpower.

Who *was* this Jerry?

Peter had a lot of experience on golf courses. He wasn't easily rattled. He remembered that the strategy for match play can be slightly different than for the more common stroke play. He knew what he had to do. But he couldn't shake the strange feeling from his bones. Again, he asked himself, who was this guy that he drew such a crowd? He couldn't help but be just a little put out by all the attention being showered on his opponent.

Then, when Jerry began to wave at the onlookers between holes, Peter could contain his curiosity no longer.

"I guess you're famous," he said quietly. "You've got quite a few fans over there. I've never seen anything like it. Are you some kind of local celebrity?"

The man grinned. "I should say so," he replied. "I live in this community."

Not only did Peter Wegmann eventually win the championship, but he also gained a valuable lesson. Never, ever let an opponent—not to mention his fan club—get to you.

13
TEACHING THE HOLOCAUST

In 1994, the Florida legislature passed SB 660, the Holocaust Education Bill, which required every one of the state's schools to teach the history of the Nazi destruction of Jews, as well as homosexuals, the disabled, Roma (aka Gypsies) and others during the Second World War. Seventeen states currently mandate some form of Holocaust education, but only eight actually have statutes on the books specifically requiring or recommending it as part of the state education curriculum.

Florida is one of only three states, however, that require K–12 genocide education and have a state commission or task force to keep the curriculum comprehensive and up to date. Surprising, then, that it was a Boca Raton high school principal who was recently investigated—and reassigned—for telling a mother of a student that he couldn't take a stand on whether or not the Holocaust actually occurred.

Before 1939, 9.5 million Jews lived in Europe. Six years later, 6 million had been murdered. More than seventy years after the war's end, it is believed that today, fewer than 100,000 of the survivors remain among us. Many of them have settled in South Florida. There was a time when elderly survivors were regularly seen in the streets of Miami Beach; since the beach's revival into a place for hipsters to see and be seen, they are more often scattered in retirement communities throughout the region.

I met Samuel Ron, born Shmuel Rakowski, several years ago, when I was hired to do some storytelling education at his luxurious senior community on

The German words on the gates of some death camps mean "Work Sets You Free." *freeimages.com*.

the campus of the Adolph & Rose Levis Jewish Community Center in Boca Raton. He was not one of the participants in the program, but his Israeli-born wife was, and she soon brought the two of us together. Here is his story:

SHMUEL RAKOWSKI WAS BORN in Kazimierza-Wielka, about fifteen miles outside of Krakow, Poland, in 1924. In the early 1940s, his family lived briefly in the city's Jewish ghetto. He then spent several months in Plaszow, the forced-labor camp featured in the film *Schindler's List*, before being shipped to several other camps. The story of Oskar Schindler is personal to Sam, because his uncles, aunt and cousin were on the list that enabled them to work at Schindler's factory, where conditions were tolerable. Sam was liberated from a Nazi death march by the U.S. Army in 1945. After liberation, he participated in the creation of the Bericha, an organization that facilitated the escape of Holocaust survivors from Eastern Europe.

Sam Ron is one of those survivors who feels that part of his life's mission is to tell the story of his experiences, as well as the experiences of those left behind in the ashes of Europe. Indeed, some survivors believe that their lives were spared for just this purpose. For fifty years, he has told his story, whether in Canton, Ohio, in Germany and Poland, in Israel or in his current home in South Florida. Even at age ninety-five, he still visits schools as part of the state's educational mandate.

Every year, the private Pine Crest School based in Boca Raton and Fort Lauderdale invites Holocaust survivors to speak to students. The children prepare for the meetings with lectures and readings in their English and social science classes and by watching the movies *Schindler's List* and, this

"I'm Really Proud of You, Dad": People and Places

year, *The Boy in the Striped Pajamas*. The program is developed by the school's Institute for Civic Involvement.

On one particularly balmy morning in January 2018, Sam was met at the door of his building by a sleek black limousine. He knew the drill, having done it so many times before. At the Fort Lauderdale campus, he met Pine Crest faculty and students who ushered him in to breakfast as if he were a rock star. Some pelted him with questions; others simply stared, or smiled, or both. Afterward, a parent and teacher stayed in the room along with the waiting class of twenty-one teenagers.

Sam began his story slowly, as always, his heavy accent and intense topic forcing the students to focus on every word. He didn't emphasize facts and figures, numbers of deaths or dates. What he tried to convey was how it felt to be hungry, really starving, for eight months. What it was like to take four separate rides in airless, stuffed cattle cars without knowing if you were going to be killed at the end of each trip.

When he had completed his story, the teacher asked if there were any questions.

"So you were actually in those places in the movie?"

"Yes, I was. They re-created Plaszow, of course, but the movie was shot in Krakow, in Poland, and just outside the gates of the concentration camp Auschwitz."

A slight, fair-skinned girl raised her hand. Sam pointed to her.

"Yes, miss? You have a question?"

"Do you still believe in God after what happened to you? And if so, how? I know I wouldn't." There was a general murmuring around the room.

"Well I tell you," Sam replied, "different survivors reacted in different ways. I am a religious person, although I go to a Reform temple, which means it's not very strict when it comes to observing the commandments. But your question of how I can believe, that's controversial, and I don't think it's right to discuss it here. All I can tell you is that I don't blame God for the bad in this world or credit Him for the good. He does what He does. He has His business, and I have mine."

At the end of the presentation, the parents and teachers led the teenagers in a standing ovation. They surrounded him afterward for additional questions, hugs, handshakes and more than a few autographs.

Sam went on to the next class, ate lunch in the cafeteria and finally took the limo home. He kissed his wife when he entered the apartment.

"How did it go?" she asked, as usual.

His response was also standard. "Fine. It went just fine."

About a week later, Sam received a packet of letters from the school. The director of the program wrote in part, "Your willingness to open your heart and tell your story opened the minds of everyone who heard it. It was a very special day, and one that our young people will never forget."

A student wrote, "I could never imagine being able to go a day without food, much less two and a half weeks."

Another: "I could imagine a twenty-year-old in thin pajamas in the shivering cold. I could imagine you being separated from your mother and father and brother.…Thank you for sharing your story and opening my perspective about the Holocaust."

And there was more.

- *I could not imagine surviving in the camps, and the fact that you were not only able to survive but bravely share your story almost half a century later inspired me to embrace my heritage even more than I already do.*
- *You told my classmates and I that your dignity was taken away. I think it is amazing that with everything that you have been through in your lifetime you are able to stay positive.*
- *One thing I really took away from your experience is that even when you thought hope was lost, you never gave up. I feel that is a lesson that should stand true for everyone.*
- *Speaking to you and hearing your story was an incredible experience that I'll likely carry with me for the rest of my life.…You are truly an amazing person and I applaud you again for being able to speak to us about such a tragedy.*
- *I could have sat in that room for hours with you, asking you a million questions.…Thank you beyond words.*
- *After hearing your experience, I have committed myself to helping and doing everything in my power to help preserve, protect and defend human rights of everybody.…It made me realize that it is our responsibility as humans to prevent history from repeating and to teach future generations about the suffering faced by the Holocaust.*

That afternoon, Sam sat at his dining room table and scanned every letter, as he had done with hundreds upon hundreds of others over the years. Every once in a while, he passed one over to his wife.

"Look at this one, Bilha," he said. "A real poet."

At the end of the evening, the elderly Holocaust survivor stood up, filed the letters away and prepared for bed. After all, tomorrow was a long day. He had an appointment to speak at another school. And another one the day after that, and one after that, and one after that.

Part 2
"IT'S A COPPER WHOPPER!"

WATER AND WEATHER

14
THE FLATSMASTER

Sure, there's fishing in plenty of states. But according to the Florida Fish and Wildlife Conservation Commission, Florida is the fishing capital of the world. Hence, I bring you a fishing story. But not just any fishing story.

If you've never heard the term *FlatsMaster*, you're not alone. For those in the know, however, it's the name of Florida's largest backcountry fishing tournament series, held in Punta Gorda, about half an hour's drive northwest from Fort Myers on the state's southwest coast. (The fame of this championship has led to its name on boats and rods, as well.) Anglers catch redfish, snook, tarpon, trout and other saltwater fish in shallow water, aka flats. Each year's winner is a FlatsMaster, according to flatsmaster.com.

It takes some skill to fish, and it takes some special kind of skill to fish the flats. Apparently, it's not so easy to sneak up on a fish in shallow water. To be successful, the flats fisherman has to be able to read the air and wind conditions, the water temperature and clarity, the flats themselves, the angle of the sun and, of course, the life beneath the water.

This story takes place on Marco Island, a barrier island in the Gulf of Mexico, about eighty miles south of Punta Gorda. It has impressive claims to fame: crystalline beaches, stunning golf courses and resort hotels, marinas and its proximity, by bridge, to Naples. Oh, and it's a great place to go flats fishing.

My former college student Anthony Armonda shared this story of his transformation as a fisherman for my Public Storyteller radio segment—and when I heard it, I said it would be a perfect addition to this book. Here is my retelling.

Florida has been dubbed the "Fishing Capital of the World." *Jacek Freyer, freeimages.com.*

ANTHONY WAS A YOUNG man who loved to fish. Growing up on the east coast of Florida, however, he had mostly been a deep-sea fisherman. Fishing in shallow water was a whole different kettle of fish and, he felt, not really in his league. Which isn't to say it wasn't one of his favorite things to do. It was. He simply enjoyed it despite its not really being so into *him*.

So it was that when Anthony's friend Pete received an invitation from *his* friend Rascal to fish the flats in Marco Island, Anthony was psyched. He'd heard dozens of stories from Pete about Rascal's prowess as a flats fisherman. He'd seen what must have been hundreds of pictures of Rascal's amazing catches. Anthony was hoping for some pointers. So was Pete. For a while, it was all the two talked about.

The pair took off at five o'clock one morning, making the two-hour drive in time to watch the sunrise. Rascal, apparently not quite as eager, joined them a little later. The three set about loading the car with fishing gear for the boat, which belonged to Rascal's dad, who lived on the island.

By the time they set off in the small craft, Rascal's enthusiasm was as high as that of the others. At one point, Anthony spotted a dolphin that was keeping pace with them off the starboard side. He pulled out his phone to get a video.

"This dolphin is definitely a good omen," he shouted to no one in particular. "This is so cool! It's gonna be a great day."

No sooner were the words out of his mouth than he felt his heart sink. He recognized the devastating signs of red tide, the periodic plague of toxic algae, just ahead. Lifeless, bloated fish had floated to the surface, bobbing on their sides at the small boat's approach. It's a painful sight for anyone, and especially an angler.

But Anthony's excitement was too high for him to be discouraged for long. The group found a quiet spot, and as soon as they got themselves situated, they all three cast their lines.

Pete hooked first, but he lost the fish within minutes. It didn't matter. That meant the fish were biting, and that was all the young men needed so early in the game.

Then Anthony noticed that Rascal kept looking over at his casting. He didn't say anything, but the more experienced flats fisherman was clearly nervous about his skill. He tried not to let it rattle him. He kept at it, watching the others from time to time, and before long, he got the hang of it.

Still, they didn't get lucky. Rascal suggested they try one of his favorite fishing spots, known as Trout Spot. They made five passes on it, but none of them caught a thing.

Rascal scratched his head. "I don't get it," he said. "I'm really stumped. The conditions are perfect here. Let's try somewhere else."

Anthony and Pete looked at each other and shrugged. Rascal was the expert. They went on to another area, where the water was a little deeper.

"The water's moving here," Rascal explained. "That's good, on a hot day like today. The fish get more oxygen."

What did they know? It certainly sounded plausible. Once again, Pete hooked first, and this one made it into the boat. It was a trout, and it was a keeper. He put it in the box. The three quietly high-fived one another.

Then Anthony felt a tug on his line, at last. *It's about time*, he thought, reaching up just for a moment to wipe the sweat from his forehead. He hadn't wanted to let it show, but he had been beginning to worry. The trout he caught was perfect.

In minutes, Rascal also caught a trout, and for the next twenty minutes or so, the group felt like they could do no wrong. It was one of those magical times when the fish seemed to be jumping into the boat of their own accord.

Anthony could have happily stayed there for the rest of the day, but Rascal had other plans. He moved the boat about ten feet down.

Anthony's first cast was perfect, if he did say so himself. It landed exactly where he'd aimed it, directly under the mangroves. As soon as it did, a fish jumped on it. He grabbed his line and the reel started to scream, one of the most beautiful sounds in the world to an angler. Then the line started ripping through the water. The fish was jumping, dancing, almost. When Anthony maneuvered it to the side of the boat, he heard Rascal's sharp intake of breath.

"Look at that! It's a Copper Whopper!"

It was Anthony's first redfish in a lifetime of angling. Not to mention his first flats fish. He felt as jubilant, he recollected later, as a kid at Christmas. But the fight wasn't over yet. As soon as he set his net into the water, the fish darted off for its last run. He held on and after a few tense minutes, brought it back and netted it.

The slot, he knew, was seventeen to twenty-eight inches. He measured his catch, and it was a keeper. He could barely contain his joy. In the next hour, he went on to catch eleven more fish, including a baby Goliath grouper, a protected species, so he threw it back. Meanwhile his friends caught just five between them.

"You've sure got the hot rod today!" Pete called out.

"Don't I know it!"

Rascal took them to one more spot, a little more secluded than the rest. As soon as Anthony cast off, he hooked a mangrove snapper. While he was reeling it in, a snook grabbed it in its mouth, so now he was reeling in the snook. He was thrilled at his luck. Before he could do much more, however, the snook started to jump and spat out the snapper.

"Copper Whopper. Goliath grouper. Mangrove snapper. And now snook!" Rascal whistled. "That would've been an in-shore grand slam! Too bad!"

Anthony shrugged. He baited the jig with shrimp and cast off right where he'd lost the snook. Sure enough, it took the bait once more. Again, the fish was jumping—then everything became a blur for Anthony. The fish ran, and his heart jumped. Using all his strength and patience, he managed to get it into the boat at last. A quick measurement told him it was thirty-one inches, safely in the slot. The only trouble? It was out of season. Never mind; he was used to catch and release. He threw it back.

The three noticed almost simultaneously that it was getting late and the weather was changing. In fact, it had already started to pour.

"Did you bring rain gear?" he called over to Pete.

"Nope. You?"

"I always do. You never know about the rain here."

On the two-mile ride back, the weather worsened, and they sailed blind after about a quarter of a mile. At last they made it back to the marina. Pete changed into dry clothes. Rascal cleaned the fish, while Anthony took care of the boat.

They didn't talk much during their work. But at one point, Rascal approached him.

"Twelve fish!" he cried out, pounding him on the shoulder. "It's true! You really *are* the FlatsMaster!"

Maybe it wasn't official, but still, it was a name he'd thought he'd never earn. And coming from Rascal, it was almost as good as coming from the tournament officials. That could wait. At least till next year.

15

THE COSTUME MUST GO ON

I've known Patricia Burdett for about fifteen years, since I started producing a storytelling series at Boca Raton's beloved Caldwell Theatre Company, where she had worked at that point for decades. Maybe the fact that Pat hails from Winnipeg, Canada, gives her an insight into some of the special challenges inherent in running a theater, or anything else, in Florida.

The theater, known originally as the Caldwell Playhouse, was to earn over the years the nicknames South Florida's "Cinderella Theater" and Boca Raton's "Jewel in the Crown." It was named for Rubbermaid founder James R. Caldwell, a prominent Boca Raton retiree who in 1975 talked the college into donating space to house the area's first professional regional theater. (Ever used a rubber dustpan? Thank Mr. and Mrs. Caldwell.) The new venue struggled at first, due in part to its location on the then-sleepy little road named Military Trail—now a major north–south artery. But just four years after opening its doors, the Caldwell earned a prestigious Carbonell Award and, at least as important, three thousand subscribers.

When the college eventually needed its space back, the theater relocated to the Boca Raton Mall—now the site of tony Mizner Park. By the time the shopping center was razed in 1989, the Caldwell was recognized as one of Florida's four state theaters. It moved to a shopping center on U.S. 1; then a new home was built for it on the adjoining lot. Before succumbing to the economic slowdown of 2012, the theater played host to up to fifty thousand patrons annually, as well as award-winning local actors and major stars like Edward Asner and Charles Nelson Reilly.

"It's a Copper Whopper!": Water and Weather

The Caldwell Theatre Company was established in 1975. *Courtesy of Caldwell Theatre Company.*

Knowing Pat as I do, it isn't a bit surprising that for thirty years or so, people who worked with her assumed that she would take care of everything. She even helped take care of this book by contributing a story.

COMPANY MANAGER PATRICIA BURDETT was used to working miracles at the Caldwell Theatre Company. Almost since the day Michael Hall and Frank Bennett opened its doors, the cast, crew and office staff alike knew one line by heart: "Don't worry; Pat will take care of it." And take care of it she always did, from last-minute publicity issues to housing to transportation to props to costumes to tickets to anything and everything.

Late one April in the late 1980s, the company presented a five-week run of a satirical comedy by the great British playwright George Bernard Shaw. Called *Misalliance*, the play, which debuted about 1910, is set in the Surrey, England conservatory of the country house of a man named John Tarleton. The action takes place all in one afternoon in late May 1909. A typical speech from the period piece goes like this:

> *Johnny: No: you don't run away. I'm going to have this out with you. Sit down: d'y' hear?* [Bentley attempts to go with dignity. Johnny slings him into a chair at the writing table, where he sits, bitterly humiliated, but afraid to speak lest he should burst into tears]. *That's the advantage of having more body than brains, you*

see: it enables me to teach you manners; and I'm going to do it too. You're a spoilt young pup; and you need a jolly good licking. And if you're not careful you'll get it: I'll see to that next time you call me a swine.

Modern, it isn't.

The revival at the Caldwell started off well, both onstage and off. Tickets sold at a good clip, and reviews were mainly favorable. The company got along great, and two of the cast members, one of whom played a character named Gunner, took a particular shine to each other and soon became a couple.

Hired from New York City just for the run of the show, neither of the lovers had been able to enjoy the sun during the long northern winter. Traditionally, theaters are dark on Mondays, so, just like any other tourists, the two young actors went off to the beach. They were both in their late twenties, fit and agile. They were undoubtedly looking forward to a long, lovely afternoon in paradise. They had undoubtedly never before encountered the searing Florida spring sun.

About half an hour before show time on that Tuesday night, Pat was checking on a few things when she noticed some of the backstage crew laughing. Always one for a good joke, she approached the open dressing room door where a number of people had congregated. What she found was a first, even for a seasoned veteran of the theater.

There stood the young man cast as Gunner, wincing and attempting in vain to stifle his agonized moans. Several other cast members, meanwhile, were wrapping long gauze bandages around his arms and across his chest and back, all of which were burned the fiery red of a rare steak.

Pat stopped dead in her tracks, surveyed the scene, and forced herself to take a couple of deep, long breaths to keep calm.

"What's going on here?" she asked.

"Uh, we were out in the sun," the actor answered, staring down at the dressing room floor as if in urgent search of a pin. It was hard to tell whether his face was redder from sunburn or from shame. Pat looked over at his friend, whose skin, though much better, was nevertheless a fetching shade of pink.

"I can see that," Pat said. "You know we have no understudy for this role, right?"

"That's why we're bandaging him," one of the other men said. "He can't wear his costume."

"Excuse me?"

"It's a Copper Whopper!": Water and Weather

The young sunbather with the bandages looked up for the first time. Pat couldn't help feeling sorry for him; his skin had to hurt like nobody's business.

"I'm not going to be able to wear the costume without these bandages," he explained. "I'm not going to be comfortable onstage. In fact, that's putting it mildly. It's going to friggin' kill me, to tell you the truth."

Pat saw the problem immediately. The men's elegant Edwardian costumes were tight-fitting vests, trousers, shirts and jackets, topped off with well-tied cravats. It was painful just to imagine wrapping all that cotton and wool around sunburned skin. As company manager, however, she had a duty to register her displeasure.

"Do you see why going out in the sun during the run may not have been the best idea?" she asked, hands on her hips. "Do you see why I specifically told you not to do it—although I knew you would anyway?" The young man hung his head a bit lower, like a chastened schoolboy. "Even if you can make it through the show without screaming," she continued, "you're not exactly going to look like an English country gentleman with that lobster-colored skin."

"I know," the actor said. "And I'm sorry. I'm really sorry. I had no idea how strong the sun was. What do I know about the beach in April? I'm a New Yorker."

There was so much she could have replied to that line. It was tempting, but instead, Pat walked out of the dressing room, shaking her head. When she was well out of earshot, however, she burst into giggles.

Amazingly, the performance went off perfectly, and only someone who had seen the production several times before would have noticed the unusual care that Gunner took in moving every muscle.

Reflecting later that night on the near-fiasco, Pat consoled herself with the thought that the situation could have been a lot worse. They could have been doing the play *Bent* that season, for instance, which contained scenes that would have put the actor's bright red chest, back, arms and legs on display for all to see. And after all, she supposed, the show was intended to demonstrate some of Shaw's ideas about the importance of physical fitness. She was just thankful it was a comedy.

She was also thankful that for once, no one had dared to say, "Don't worry; Pat will take care of it."

16

HOW ONE NEW YORKER CAME TO LOVE FLORIDA

This story brings up an attitude I have encountered several times in the state, although to my knowledge, it is primarily a South Florida phenomenon. Over the past fifty years, this region has been the victim—or beneficiary, depending on your point of view—of rampant development. Huge swaths of wetlands and farmland have been paved over, and gated communities and shopping centers permeate the once predominantly wild landscape. This means that sometimes, unless you know where to look, South Florida can appear to be one big concrete jungle. And for those former New Yorkers or Canadians who don't make it north of Palm Beach or south of Miami, it may seem like that's all there is to the state.

Case in point: As Dr. Holly Larson and I were discussing her experience, I recalled that the first time I encountered the Everglades, I didn't know what I was seeing. I could understand why this one-of-a-kind ecosystem would have looked like nothing to state leaders but a lot of muck to be dredged to turn it into something useful. Sometimes it is only when we come to know a place that we see its beauty, vibrancy and value.

In this story, Holly shares the limelight with threadfin herring, also known as greenbacks, or greenies. These are scaly fish found in deep water, typically used for bait for tarpon, redfish and other catch. They are about two to five inches in length, have a (predictably) dark green back, dark spots along the dorsal ridge and a long thread of a fin. To my knowledge, no one has ever reported a spiritual experience with them. Until now.

"It's a Copper Whopper!": Water and Weather

Swimming in the midst of a school of fish can be magical. *Oktaviani Marvikasari, freeimages.com*.

I met Holly twenty years ago, when she had just returned from a U.S. Peace Corps posting overseas. Being a former Peace Corps volunteer myself, I felt an immediate kinship with her. But I hadn't heard this story before I started to write this book. And here you think you know a person.

Holly Larson hated Florida, and she didn't care who knew it. It was early September 1998, and she had spent the summer with her mother and sister in Coconut Creek, a place she had visited regularly since her grandparents moved there more than two decades earlier. She was happy to be making some money teaching GED courses at a local high school and, for the first time in her life, was seriously considering education as a career. Having returned from the Peace Corps with barely five dollars in her pocket, Holly felt that her mother's invitation to stay rent-free for a few months had been a godsend.

After a very short time in the state, however, she realized that she had made a terrible mistake. This was not the Florida she remembered. She still had visions of picking sweet strawberries in fragrant fields and pausing to watch grazing horses and cattle. But that was then, and this was now. Now all she saw were shopping malls and highways. Not to mention the fact that this was the first time she had been down here in the summer months, and the humidity was killing her. She would just recover from one sinus infection when she came down with another. And to add insult to injury, her body had long been acclimated to the cold—even on the coast of Morocco, where she'd just spent two years. Before that, it was upstate New York where she'd gone to school, or Long Island, where she grew up. Air-conditioning just didn't come close.

"This sucks," she told her mother, one eighty-degree morning. "I've got to get out of here and get back to New York. It's not that I don't appreciate being here with you. I really do. But I can't stand Florida anymore. It's nothing like what I remember as a kid."

Her mother looked at her younger daughter, her lips pursed in sympathy. "Tell you what," she said. "Let's go to the west coast. For a treat."

Holly's eyes lit up. "California?"

"No, silly, I'm talking about the west coast of Florida. Sarasota. I've got a timeshare." At the change in Holly's expression, she added, "It's beautiful there. Museums, the Gulf, lots to see and do. It's more like old Florida. You'll love it."

She wasn't completely convinced, but the following week, Holly, her mother and her sister Hope drove several hours across the state. As soon as they arrived, she had to admit that she did like it better than where she'd been living lately. It felt calmer. More natural. More like the Florida she remembered.

The women had heard that the best snorkeling on the Gulf Coast could be found off Siesta Key, about fifteen minutes southwest of Sarasota. There was also great birding, shelling, kayaking, nurse sharks, fishing for snook and snapper—all the things that would take Holly's mind off big-box stores and traffic jams.

A popular attraction on Siesta Key is Point of Rocks, a rare geological phenomenon consisting of a series of limestone rock formations. On the southern end of the beach on Siesta Key, Point of Rocks boasts ledges that reach out more than a hundred yards into the Gulf. And the water is supposed to be so clear that sometimes you can see as much as twenty feet down.

The three settled on blankets not far from the Siesta Key Pavilion. They chatted. They ate sandwiches. They lounged in the sun, which was not as blazing as it had seemed to be on the east coast. Then Holly announced that she was going to take a run along the beach.

Two miles down, she stopped. There was no mistaking it after having seen its picture: Point of Rocks. She slowed her pace and walked in the direction of the water. She was overheated. More importantly, she was curious. It was a perfect time, and place, for a swim.

Holly waded into the warm water and began the smooth, slow, even strokes of the front crawl. *Ah,* she thought, *this is the life. This makes up for a lot.*

She had been swimming for a few minutes when she felt something, a tickle, a flutter, a strange, not altogether unpleasant sensation on her legs. She lowered her face into the Gulf and experienced such a deep intake of breath she had to raise her head and spit out water. What had she seen? Was it a cloud? She lowered her face again and saw, to her amazement, a school of tiny green fish. There were thirty or forty of them, each about the size of her ring finger.

They were floating around her, encircling her, as if they were inviting her to come along. As if she were one of them.

Her first feeling was fright. She was a New Yorker, after all. What did she know about swimming with fish? But they were bouncing off her body, gently poking her arms and legs, as if—she knew it was a funny thing to imagine, but as if they were inviting her to play.

For fifteen minutes, Holly swam with the greenbacks, and her initial fear melted into a delight she had never experienced before. For the first time in her life, she felt like she was a part of nature. Like there was no barrier between her and the natural world.

When the fish finally swam on without her, Holly felt disappointed, but only for a moment. She knew she had just had the kind of meaningful, spiritual experience that would stay with her forever.

And indeed, that swim with the greenbacks changed not only Holly's perspective about Florida, but also the rest of her life. She remained in the state and began to tour and learn about it on outings with Florida Humanities. She fell in love with the natural areas, history and culture. She returned to school, earned her doctorate and eventually settled into a tenured position at Seminole State College, in Sanford, half an hour northeast of Orlando. Through it all, she made a point to return to Siesta Key to swim with the fish nearly every year.

And to this day, she'll tell anyone who'll listen that sometimes, you've got to really pay attention to fall in love.

17

WHY DID THE MANATEE CROSS THE ROAD?

Hurricanes tend to be an unhappy feature of Florida life, but to paraphrase Tolstoy, each of them is unhappy in its own way. From August 9 to 15, 2004, Hurricane Charley attacked the state's southwest, making landfall with winds of 150 miles per hour. It was one of the strongest such storms to ever hit the United States and the worst in that part of Florida since 1960. Afterward, residents of the area began to talk about their lives in terms of pre-Charley and post.

Laurie Martin and her family sat out the storm in their little two-story home on Fort Myers Beach, a sugar sand paradise on the north end of Estero Island on Florida's southwest coast. I was introduced to Laurie by telephone after meeting her neighbor Russ when I performed at the beautiful Fort Myers Beach Library. "You want a great only-in-Florida story?" he asked me. "You've got to talk to Laurie Martin." When he sketched the outline of it, I couldn't wait to talk to her.

Spoiler alert: The Martins, thankfully, survived the storm just fine. This story is about surviving parents.

When you've lived in an area twenty years, and you've gone through your share of hurricanes, you think you know what to expect. Besides, evacuation is a mess. Not only do you hit the highway with thousands of other cars, but you also have no way of defending your home against nature—or vandals. What's more, at one time on Fort Myers Beach, you couldn't return after

"It's a Copper Whopper!": Water and Weather

Mariners and fishermen used to think manatees were mermaids. *David Sinofksy, freeimages.com.*

the storm until everything had been officially evaluated for safety, which added considerably to the general confusion and disorientation, not to mention expense, of displaced homeowners. So when the area was placed under mandatory evacuation in advance of Hurricane Charley, and Laurie Martin's mother told her she was concerned about her staying in the house, Laurie told her she had everything under control.

"We're evacuating, Mom," she said. "Don't worry." The phone was tucked between her shoulder and her ear, making it tough to put up the shutters on the windows.

"Because you know if there's a problem, either before or after the storm, how will you get off the island? And Hannah's just three. She'll be really scared by all that wind!"

"You're absolutely right, Mom. We're leaving as soon as we can. Look, I'll call you later. Gotta get packed up."

But Laurie and her husband had no intention of evacuating. They tested out their generator, stocked up on gas, water and food. When the hurricane roared in around one or two o'clock in the afternoon, the house was well anchored down, and the next-door neighbors had come by to ride out the storm on their comfortable second floor. At one point during the night, the water began to rise as the back bay and beachfront surged together. When it reached the mailbox, Laurie found herself second-guessing their decision. But then it began to subside, and she breathed easier. The couples enjoyed good food and more than a few bloody Marys. Linda stood out on the deck watching the crazy weather till the wind got too strong. All in all, they sustained only a little roof damage.

Little Hannah, meanwhile, slept through it all.

When it was over, they went downstairs to clean out the sand and the dirt on the floors and elsewhere, including bleaching anything that might get moldy. Laurie found an enormous leatherback turtle that must have come in from the pond in the nearby plaza. Carefully, they eased it back where it belonged.

The island was without power for five days, but between the National Guard and the Red Cross, they were in pretty good shape. It was strange, though, watching the odd objects floating past in the bay. Mats. Parts of a roof. Refrigerators and stoves. Then there was the panicked barking of dogs left behind in otherwise abandoned houses. Because the storm had not been forecast to do much damage to the area, residents had been instructed to leave them in bathrooms with food and water for just two days.

At one point, Laurie's husband said he was going a little stir-crazy.

"I think I'll take a swim down the road," he announced one morning. "Wanna come along?"

"I don't think that's such a good idea," Laurie said. Her next-door neighbors concurred. "You never know what you'll find floating out there."

"I'll be careful," he said with a shrug. "Come with me if you're worried."

"Okay. Why don't we all go?"

The swim went without incident, and afterward, the group walked down the beach to survey the damage. Flotsam and jetsam were everywhere.

At one point, someone noticed smoke billowing out from nearby Pearl Street. The couples rushed over to find a burning house and their friend Russ hosing down his property next door to keep the flames from getting too close. It was sad, but there was no way around it. The house had to burn to the ground. The fire department couldn't get through due to the mandatory evacuation.

They were just a few blocks from their home when they found something even stranger. They saw a small crowd of locals gathering around a canal on Ohio Street. When the neighbors drew closer, they realized to their shock that a manatee had washed up on the road.

It's no wonder that sailors used to think that manatees were mermaids. The creatures, also known as sea cows, are huge and oddly human-like. This one was just a baby, maybe six feet in length, but it still weighed hundreds of pounds. It regarded them all with a sad, intelligent expression, as if it were sorry for putting them out.

"What should we do?" someone asked. "How do we get something that big back into the water?"

One of their friends ran home to get supplies. But how were they going to keep the magnificent creature wet, and calm, until the man returned? From out of nowhere, it seemed, someone appeared with a handful of buckets. One by one, the people who had gathered there climbed down the nearest boat ramp, filled the buckets, and returned to pour water on the manatee and rub it into its skin. It was such an amazing experience that someone recorded the incident on her cellphone.

At last, the friend returned with a large sheet of plywood, a length of heavy rope attached to one end. The growing crowd managed to coax the manatee onto the plywood, hook the rope to the man's truck and drag it to the water, at which point the manatee did the rest of the job itself.

It was memorable, to be sure, but a week later, in the midst of the last residual bits of hurricane cleanup, Laurie forgot about it. Until, that is, her mother called.

"So you're lying to your mother now, are you?" These were the first words Laurie heard when she picked up the phone.

"Of course not! What do you mean?"

"You didn't evacuate at all, did you?"

"Mom, why would you say that?"

"Because I saw your picture! I saw your picture in the paper with that manatee!"

Laurie's jaw dropped. She remembered the neighbor with the camera.

"What are you talking about? That picture just had hands on it! What makes you think it was me?"

"What, are you kidding me? I'd recognize your hand anywhere!"

Laurie looked down at her hand, and then she realized what her mother meant. It was her engagement ring. The stone had come from her husband's family, but she had designed the setting herself, Portuguese gold, because her mother is Portuguese.

"You got me, Mom," she said after a long pause. "I'm sorry. I just didn't want you to worry. Are you mad?"

"I'm not mad at all," her mother said. "I'm relieved that you were all spared. But just remember for next time. You may be able to fool Mother Nature, but you can never, ever fool your mother."

18

THERE'S NO PLACE LIKE HOME

As we've seen already, it's impossible to write about Florida without writing about hurricanes. Lots of hurricanes. And some of the most interesting hurricane stories are from people who actually missed them. Case in point: Pat Nease was on the opposite side of the state—425 miles away from her home in Panama City—when she got the news about what misery Hurricane Michael, which made landfall in the Florida Panhandle on October 10, 2018, was bringing her family and neighbors. The storm, which turned out to be a Category 5 (winds greater than 155 miles per hour), cost at least seventy-four deaths and more than $25 billion.

Pat is a professional storyteller, and I had hired her to perform a show at the Boca Raton Public Library in Palm Beach County the weekend of the storm. Prior to that show, she had scheduled an in-service training at the Broward County Library Southwest Regional Branch. Between the two dates, her life, and most of all her home, were transformed. (Not to mention the fact that I had to hire a replacement for her show.)

When Pat Nease left her house for the long drive to South Florida, she knew a hurricane was on its way to the Panhandle. But the news reports said it would be a Category 1 or 2, which meant wind speeds of "only" maybe up to 110 miles per hour. And besides, hurricanes can veer off course. So, she thought, no big deal. After all, she had grown up in Florida, and she'd lived in the area for thirty-plus years. She knew hurricanes. What's more,

"It's a Copper Whopper!": Water and Weather

The damage caused by hurricanes can be not only physical but also emotional. *Palmer W. Cook, freeimages.com.*

the house was strong; they had good hurricane shutters, they'd carried in all the outdoor furniture, and as if that weren't enough, their property was eighteen feet above the bay. So at least they didn't have to worry about storm surge.

So Pat set off on the long road trip thinking about the stories she was going to tell in Palm Beach County, the workshop for the librarians she had set for Thursday, anything but the weather. They had lived through storms so many times before; they would live through storms so many times to come. Her attitude was the epitome of "been there, done that."

On October 9, Pat stopped off at the house of a friend in Deland, about five hours into the eight-and-a-half-hour trip. Foregoing television and Internet for the evening, the two friends enjoyed their share of wine and conversation. Then Pat set off for her final destination late Wednesday. Again, it was to be a respite with a good friend, a lovely, relaxing evening.

That night, she checked the Internet, and that's when she learned the storm had been worse than expected. But that could mean anything, right? It wasn't until 6:00 a.m. Thursday morning that Pat caught some conclusive news on the radio, and by that time, she was already preparing for the trip to the library to do the workshop.

In the car, she dialed her son, over and over, without pause. But she couldn't get through. Later, as she discussed the mechanics of storytelling with librarians, normally one of her greatest professional pleasures, her heart was in her throat, and only half of her brain was on her work. The other half was asking: Is everybody all right? Do I have a home?

After the workshop, Pat may have looked at her hostess and friend and hugged her. She doesn't remember. She just continued to call Wyatt, over and over. After all, phone lines go out for all sorts of reasons. Not getting through could mean anything!

At a certain point, she rationed herself, saying: *I'm only going to call every fifteen minutes. Every twenty. If he can call me, he will. Won't he?*

At last, after trying for six or seven hours, she picked up the call from her son. "Mom!"

She was so shocked that at first, she didn't know what to say. Then she blurted out, "Wyatt, I've been trying and trying to reach you!"

"I know. Our phone service is out. I'm using a friend's line. Oh Mom, you've got to come home. Now. We're fine, but the house—it's gone, Mom. The house is gone. You gotta come, soon as you can."

It's worth noting at this point that Pat's son was forty-four, with a reputation for being independent, capable and cool in an emergency. She had never heard his voice so broken and frightened, even when he was a child.

"I'm coming, honey," she said. "I'm on my way. Just hold on. As long as you and Dad are all right. Just hold on a little longer."

"Okay, okay. Gotta get off the phone now. Drive safe."

And with that, the line to her family was dead.

Somehow Pat had the presence of mind to remember to call and cancel her next gig. Then she said her good-byes and jumped into the car. She raced out of the Fort Lauderdale area as though it, or she, were on fire.

Tuning into a news station on the radio, it occurred to her: They're going to need food. She pulled into a Walmart, grabbed a cart and started down the aisles like she was in one of those supermarket contests in which you fill your cart with everything you can in five minutes. What will they need? Bread. Lunchmeat. Cans—peas, carrots, corn, beans—all the vegetables she realized afterward that they didn't eat. Then she thought: *We don't have a cooler!* She reached for an insulated bag. *Beer! We need beer!*

By the time Pat checked out, her bill was well over $200, and she had been in the store all of fifteen minutes. She packed everything into the car as best she could. By the time she turned north for the long haul to Panama City, it was 3:00 p.m.

"It's a Copper Whopper!": Water and Weather

Left with nothing but her fears, she called her daughter in Minnesota. She answered on the first ring.

"Mom," her daughter said, "it's awful, what I'm seeing on the news. The electricity is down! There's looting at the Dollar Store! And gas, Mom, be sure you get gas!"

From then on, every time the gas needle dropped a hair, Pat pulled into a station. She had no choice. There was no way of knowing how quickly nearby stations would be depleted.

The last time she pulled off the road, she added a dozen doughnuts to her gas purchase. Fuel, she reflected, comes in all varieties.

And then, after dark, she saw the first trees lying on their sides as though broken in pieces by a giant hand.

The phone rang. "Mom," her daughter said, "They've blockaded 231 and 79. Plus route 77. You can't get in. I'm telling you—you'd better pull over for the night."

"How well do you know your mother, dear? I'm going home. Whatever it takes."

After she clicked off the phone, Pat's mind raced with possibilities. The small town of Wewahitchka is about thirty miles from Panama City, at the junction of Routes 71 and 22. Take 22 west, she knew, and you're home free.

"I'll just get off the interstate at 231 and sneak in through Wewakitchka," she said aloud.

The headlights of her car were the only lights for miles. Trees were sprawled every which way across the road. At the turn-off to Route 22, the road sign was down, so she passed it before realizing what she'd done. For the first and probably last time in her life, she simply cut across the median to circle back.

The closer she got, the more she felt the fear creep up her spine. She was afraid she'd get stuck or run over an animal. Or worse. Then she saw her exit. And with it, the full effect of the wreckage hit her. Downed trees covered the road. Buildings that she'd known in Lynn Haven, a small town just outside Panama City, had vanished. It was like an out-of-body experience, that dark road, that mass destruction, but she kept driving. She knew she was heading home, but at the same time, she didn't know exactly where she was with so few landmarks.

At one point she saw the flashing lights of a police car. She slowed down, pulled out her license, but, amazingly, the officers ignored her, preferring to continue their coffee drinking and conversation. *Okay*, she thought, *I'm all right!* Soon she came upon more police cars and lights, but once again, she passed right on through.

She thought she was passing the intersection of 98 and Twenty-Third Street, but she wasn't sure, there was so much wreckage. The downed power lines and poles meant she had to drive ten or fifteen miles an hour to wind her way though. At last she knew she was getting closer to Parker, her own community.

Pat's house was tucked in by the bay. There were several ways she could have gone, but they were all blocked. Not till she reached city hall did she find the roads a little clearer, and lighter, thanks to a generator inside.

She parked at city hall, took from the car a small flashlight and a box of doughnuts and started walking down Second Street to her house. Halfway down the street, however, there were so many wires that she couldn't go through. So she tried Third. Holding her breath, she crawled under, around and between downed power lines, till she reached her property.

It was dark, the dark of haunted houses and lonely midnight vigils. And the driveway overflowed with debris. Pat opened the downstairs door, only to be greeted by her son coming out of the bedroom—with a rifle.

"Don't shoot!" she said. "I have doughnuts!"

Her son looked at her in disbelief. "Mom! You made it!" He hugged her like he'd never expected to see her again.

"Hey, hey, Wyatt! It's okay."

"Mom," he said seriously, "you know I've done dangerous things all over the world. The places I've surfed, skateboarded, the horrific things I've been through. But I tell you, I've never been so scared. I thought the house was coming down on us. And it just went on and on and on like that. As it turns out, it's bashed in plenty, but it made it. It's going to be okay."

"I feel so guilty I wasn't here for it," she said. "There I was, living in the lap of luxury across the state."

"I'm glad you didn't have to suffer through this, believe me. But how in the world did you get here?"

Despite her distress, Pat grinned.

"You don't look pleased," she said. "Didn't you tell me to come? I remember your exact words: 'Mom…'"

Even in the thin light of the flashlight, she could see him flush.

"I know what I said. I'm just amazed that you made it. I know what's going on out there."

"I left the car and walked," she explained. To his shocked expression, she added, "Hey, I didn't think it would be so bad. In daylight, I might not have tried it. But you know what they say: You don't know what you don't know. The only thing I knew was that I had to get home."

19

BALLAST

You can live alongside any part of the 1,350 miles of Florida coastline without ever getting near a sailboat, but I'm not sure why you'd want to. Sailing clubs dot the state's coasts, and in South Florida, where this story is set, we have Fort Lauderdale, widely recognized as the yachting capital of the world, with fifty thousand of the crafts registered. The fifty-nine-year-old Fort Lauderdale International Boat Show is one of the world's best and largest, and its ports are regarded as equally impressive.

Beckyjo Bean lives in this marine mecca, but her story takes place in glittering Biscayne Bay, a bit farther south, in Miami. Biscayne Bay is a lagoon, as much as eight miles wide and about thirty-five miles in length, making it the largest estuary on the state's southeast coast. The bay, which is home to the enormous Biscayne National Park, among others, has been a source of inspiration and fascination for folks across the state and halfway around the world for centuries, serving as a hub for business, transit and plain old, good clean fun.

I met Beckyjo when she told another story for the Public Storyteller, and we reconnected at a monthly storytelling slam I hold in Boca Raton. The following tale earned her the grand prize.

One day in early spring, Beckyjo's good friend Rebecca told her that she had never been sailing and that she would like to go sometime.

"You've come to the right person!" Beckyjo replied. "I've been sailing since I was six years old. I even taught sailing at Disney World. If you want to sail, I'm the person to take you. It'll be great!"

ONLY IN FLORIDA

The Laser sailboat has a well-deserved reputation for speed. *Hector Landaeta, freeimages.com*.

"It's a Copper Whopper!": Water and Weather

The two friends were psyched. They proceeded to do what any red-blooded American would do in such a situation in the 2010s: they bought a Groupon. So it was that one sparkling May Sunday after church, they changed clothes and headed over to Biscayne Bay for their adventure.

The first thing they had to do on their arrival was convince the young man who was renting them the boat that they knew what they were doing.

"Have either of you sailed before?" he asked. "Do you have experience?"

"Sure," Beckyjo said promptly. "I know everything about sailing. All you have to do is remind me where the brakes are!"

When she saw the poor guy grow pale, she took pity on him.

"Just kidding!" she said quickly. "I've been sailing for over fifty years. I learned on an El Torito. Then I graduated to a sailfish, then a flying junior. At Disney, I taught people how to sail Hobie Cats. Most recently I sailed with a local club in the Fort Lauderdale area. You may know it…"

He put up his hands. "All right, all right. You pass the test. Let's take a look at the boats for you to choose."

They wandered along the dock, Rebecca trailing behind. Nothing spoke to Beckyjo until she saw the Laser, and she stopped dead.

"That's the one."

"You sure?" He squinted. "That's a pretty fast boat you got there."

"I know. It was used in the Olympics. My uncle helped design it. But I never got a chance to sail it before. I've got to try it out."

The three returned to the office, filled out some paperwork and before long, they were sailing out of the marina. Becky could feel the man's eyes on her, but she had no fear. The sun was smiling down on her shoulders, the breeze was perfect for a nice, calm sail and the boat was proving very responsive. When she checked behind her a few minutes later, she was glad to see that he had disappeared inside.

The International Laser Class sailboat is a one- or two-person sailing dinghy, among the most widely used of its kind. It boasts a reputation for durability, easy rigging and sailing and, above all, speed. Made of GLP (glass reinforced plastics) with a foam inner layer for strength, the boat weighs just 130 pounds, with a hull length of under fourteen feet. It is known to require both considerable skill as well as a heck of a lot of endurance.

Beckyjo knew some of this background, and the rest she could guess. But she was having too much fun. She maneuvered the boat with such ease that at one point she smiled to herself. It had been a while since she'd sailed, and she had to admit she had been just a tad worried. *But it's just like riding a bicycle*, she thought. *Some things you never forget, no matter how long it's been since you've done them.*

In truth, she couldn't recall how long it had been since she'd gone sailing. She didn't get around to doing a heck of a lot of physical activity these days. Over the past decades, Becky had put on a considerable amount of weight, and for quite some time now she had been tipping the scales at two hundred pounds. But being out there on the waves that day, she remembered what it was to be more agile. She hadn't felt so good in years.

She looked over at Rebecca. Tiny and dark, Rebecca sat still, her head seeming to bob with the rise and fall of the water. She hadn't talked a lot, but what she had said was punctuated with "Wow!" and "This is fantastic!" and "I can't believe how well you sail!" and other upbeat exclamations.

This was a great day, all right. They'd remember it for a long time. And who knows? Maybe they'd make a habit of it.

The two were having so much fun that it was quite some time before Beckyjo noticed how small the massive Miami skyline was looking. Then she looked up and got sight of the darkening clouds. For the first time, she realized that the wind had picked up, and the waves had grown taller and more fierce.

"Rebecca!" she called out. "I think we've got to turn around."

Rebecca frowned. "So soon?"

"Yeah, sorry, I'm afraid so. We don't necessarily have to go in yet, but we've gotten too far out, and the weather is looking a little funky." She was annoyed that she hadn't checked the weather before they'd gone out. So many things to remember!

As a seasoned sailor, Beckyjo knew there were two ways to turn a boat around. The first, coming about, is a nice, leisurely, carefully considered turn. Jibing, on the other hand, is the opposite. The sail comes across really fast, and the sailor has to run to the other side to maneuver. Everything happens really fast with jibing.

Normally, Beckyjo would have come about. She had plenty of time. But for some reason she couldn't explain, she jibed. And just like that, the little Laser went *whoosh*.

"Holy Toledo!" she cried. "Rebecca, run to the other side. Quick!"

She tried to move quickly herself. But at 200-plus pounds, there wasn't much she did quickly. Instead of a nimble sailor, she felt like an elephant lumbering across the boat.

The boat couldn't wait. It tipped over, and the two women fell into the bay.

Becky felt herself getting swept out to sea. She grabbed onto the mainsheet and held it taut in order to climb back on. Meanwhile, Rebecca caught hold of the rudder.

The sailor looked at her friend.

"It's a Copper Whopper!": Water and Weather

"Don't worry!" she said. "This is no big deal. The first thing you learn in sailing school is what to do when you capsize. I'll get us up in no time."

"Thank goodness!" her friend called back. "Because there's something I didn't tell you."

"What's that?"

"I don't know how to swim!"

Beckyjo gulped. Then she remembered. Rebecca was wearing a life jacket.

"Don't worry!" she repeated. "We're good! It's all good!"

Meanwhile, the wind was rising, and so were the waves. Beckyjo had to act. She began to crawl around the boat. Unfortunately, the bottom of the Laser is so sleek that there is nothing to hold onto. The key is to reach over the top and pull yourself around onto the boat.

She knew Rebecca was too tiny to get her arms over the side of the boat to help her get to the centerboard in the middle. So she made her way over and pulled herself up to get the boat to tip up. It didn't budge. She began to jump on the centerboard, again and again, as the wind and waves grew nastier and the sky darkened to slate.

Beckyjo knew just what to do, but she couldn't get it to work.

Meanwhile, Rebecca contributed the only thing she could: moral support.

"You're doing a great job, Beckyjo! You're amazing! You're the best! You can do this!"

It was good to hear, but she wasn't so sure she believed it. Because the more she jumped, the more exhausted she got. And she knew why she was so exhausted. It was because she was so overweight.

All she could think was: *I don't know if I can do this. And Rebecca can't hold on much longer. She's going to let go. She's going to be swept out to sea, and I'm going to have to let go and help her, because I'm certainly not going to stay here watching her drown. Then we're both going to die in the ocean. And it's all my fault. It's all because I'm so fat.*

Then Beckyjo thought of how just a few hours before, she had been sitting in church. *God*, she began to pray. *If you save us, I'll....*

She never got to articulate her bargain, because just then a beautiful fishing yacht appeared out of nowhere.

"Need some help, girls?" the captain called out.

"Yes, please!" they said in unison.

Within two minutes, the captain told them that the mainsheet was taut.

"Sailing 101," he said. "Release the mainsheet."

She did, and the boat immediately righted itself.

"I know, I know," Becky replied, almost to herself. "When you capsize, the first thing you do is release all the lines, then you go to the centerboard and stand up, the boat rights itself, you climb in and you go. I can't believe I forgot."

"It happens to us all," the captain said with a smile. "Take good care!"

And with that, the yacht disappeared in a spray of watery diamonds.

A minute later, they fell over again.

Oh no, Beckyjo thought. *This time we're doomed*!

She was about to turn to Rebecca and say, she hoped, something a bit more positive, when two Boston Whalers materialized out of the surf. As with the yacht, it seemed to the two women as though they had appeared out of thin air. At the helm of each was a young, handsome U.S. Coast Guard officer, as crisp as their white uniforms.

The men acted every bit as efficiently as Beckyjo and Rebecca could have hoped. One of them stayed with the boat; the other took them back to the marina. He tried to call the sailing club to get someone to bring in the Laser, but there was no answer.

By the time they reached the marina, the young man was back at his post, and the captain offered to take him back to pick up the boat.

The marina employee looked at Beckyjo.

"You'll stay till I get back?"

"Of course."

They were gone quite a while. Meanwhile, the two women held the towels from the Coast Guard around them as tightly as possible. It wasn't that they were so cold. They just needed—security.

"You know how we were studying the glory of God in church?" Rebecca suddenly asked at one point, as they sipped weak coffee.

"Sure. Why?"

"Don't laugh. But when I saw those two gorgeous guys come up to save us, I swear I saw the glory of God."

Beckyjo nodded. At that moment, she wondered if she'd ever smile again.

At last, the employee returned. He was soaked from head to foot.

"I didn't mean to be so long," he said sheepishly, grabbing a towel from behind the counter. "I capsized three times. It's really rough out there."

"I'm so sorry," Beckyjo said quietly.

"Well that's the thing," he went on. "One of those times, I lost my radio. It costs $150. And I was wondering…."

"Absolutely," she said. "We'll pay for it. If SeaTow had brought us in it would have been almost ten times that. There's just one thing."

"Yeah?"

"Would you give me the box it came in?"

The employee looked at her oddly, but he reached below the counter and handed her the box. Becky immediately made out a check.

"I'll give you half when we get back," Rebecca whispered.

"Thanks."

In the car on the way home, Rebecca picked up the empty box from the back seat.

"It's a reminder," Beckyjo explained to her friend, anticipating the question. "Whenever I reach for a doughnut, I will look at that box to remember how my weight almost drowned us."

"If it weren't for the glory of God," Rebecca said quietly.

Becky smiled for the first time in an hour. Then she dipped her head.

"Amen."

20

THE SPONGER AND THE SEABIRD

After finishing a job not far from Tarpon Springs on Florida's Gulf Coast, I made a long-anticipated visit to the city, parking just off the picturesque waterfront that is Dodecanese Boulevard. Here by the Historic Sponge Docks, sponge divers rub shoulders with tourists in a few-block mecca of Greek food and gift items. The scene is a dim reflection of an imported industry that arrived with immigrant spongers around the turn of the nineteenth century and was once the state's biggest business.

When I stopped in at the tourist information office to ask if there were any spongers I could interview in this "Sponge Capital of the World," I soon realized I had struck storytelling gold. The woman behind the counter sent me to a shop whose proprietor directed me to the *Anastasi*, a forty-six-foot sponge boat that was first in line at the dock, just beyond the whitewashed storefronts. Sitting in the shade watching me make my way over was Anastasios Karistinos, the boat's owner and the merchant's dad.

Anastasios, or Taso emigrated from the Greek island of Evia in the early seventies at age eighteen. His story takes place about two hours north of the city, in the Gulf of Mexico near the mouth of the Suwanee River.

The river's biggest claim to fame, incidentally, is that "Swanee River" is the unofficial name for the Stephen Foster song "Old Folks at Home," written in 1851 and recorded by Bing Crosby and numerous others. It is the official state song of Florida, now with more enlightened lyrics than those of the original.

"It's a Copper Whopper!": Water and Weather

Tarpon Springs is the undisputed "Sponge Capital of the World." *Na Nau, freeimages.com*.

The revised chorus is: "All the world is sad and dreary/Everywhere I roam. O dear ones, how my heart grows weary/Far from the old folks at home."

Fortunately, despite the inherent danger in Taso's profession—and the terror in this story—his tale is considerably more uplifting than the song. Here is my version.

ANASTASIOS KARISTINOS COMES FROM a long line of spongers in the Greek Isles. On his arrival in the United States, Tarpon Springs was not his first stop. But when he found it, he recognized it as his new home.

About a decade after he arrived, Taso was sponging with a friend of his from Turkey. Historically, the Turks and the Greeks have been at odds for at least a century, but these two were able to put aside ethnic animosities and work together. That day, Taso was in and out of the water for hours looking for new areas to harvest, while his friend manned the boat.

It was maybe half an hour before sunset, and Taso was tired. They were still a good distance offshore.

"Take off your suit and relax," his friend said. While the man steered the boat, he kept track of the sea with the depth recorder. Meanwhile, Taso took off the jacket and shoes. A sponge diver typically works in a heavy wetsuit.

With the help of an air hose on the boat, he can harvest sponges at a depth of fifty feet or more—although the Greek divers have been known to go down beyond two hundred, sometimes in a single, very long breath.

"How does it look down there?" Taso asked.

"I think I've found a nice area," his friend replied. He stopped the boat. "You want to make one more dive, just to look? You don't have to stay down there long. If you see something, we'll stay. Otherwise, we'll keep going."

"Sure, why not?"

While his friend dropped a big floating buoy to mark the spot, Taso put back on his jacket and shoes. He could feel the boat drifting a couple of hundred yards while he was getting dressed.

"Hey man," he said, "Take me back over to the buoy."

"Sure." In order to rev up the engine, he had to disengage the compressor that had been used for Taso's oxygen supply. Then he had enough speed to bring the boat back to the buoy in no time.

Taso was ready to dive. He looked at his friend and gave him a thumbs up. Everything's okay. He waited for the same signal. Then he jumped into the water.

He was wearing fifty pounds of lead to sink down as quickly as possible. Like a paratrooper jumping out of an airplane, he thought. Down, down, down.

But where was the air? That's when it hit him. The man on the boat had forgotten to switch the compressor back to deliver the oxygen! His tank had originally had about thirty pounds of psi capacity, but now it didn't even have that. And he couldn't just make his way back up. Not with the weights. He shook his head in disgust. He had no rope, either.

Trying not to panic, he reached for the valve on the right side of his facemask and turned it all the way up. Then he remembered. After the pressure sinks below twenty pounds, the oxygen shuts off automatically so as not to turn on too quickly and cause massive damage. (Think eyeballs sucked out of their sockets.)

Taso hit the sea bottom, swam up ten feet and immediately found himself pulled right back down. *Damn*, he thought. In his distress, he hadn't remembered to disengage himself from the lead weights. This time he removed the air hose from the weights and looked up at the surface. Even in a crisis, he couldn't help admiring it. It was like a mirror, reflecting the sunlight above. Up there was life. Down here was —he didn't want to think about it.

An experienced diver, Taso began to swim hard, kicking, kicking, his lungs beginning to burn. He had no air at all in his lungs when the oxygen ran out. But he couldn't take off his mask, or he would drown.

"It's a Copper Whopper!": Water and Weather

Halfway up, he stopped. The buoyancy, he knew, would push him the rest of the way. At last he hit the surface and pulled off one side of his mask. He took a deep breath and felt his heart racing like a motor. He heard the blood vessels popping—*shhhh*—on the side of his head, but it didn't bother him. It was the best buzz of his life. The only problem for the moment was that he felt so light-headed that he almost passed out.

As luck would have it, he surfaced about fifty feet from the boat. That's when his friend saw him. Taso could see the thoughts reveal themselves on his face. In a flash, the man on the boat switched on the compressor. The sponger lay there in the water with the valve wide open, luxuriating in the flow of oxygen. It took him about five minutes until he was breathing naturally. In the meantime, the boat reached him, and his friend threw out the ladder. Taso climbed up and sat in the bow, saying nothing, just staring into the water.

"I see you didn't have air for a while. That's tough, man."

Taso was so angry he couldn't find the words. He opened his mouth to yell, but he was too worn out. His friend took a long drag of his cigarette and went back to steering the boat.

But there was more than anger keeping Taso from speaking. He just sat there, thinking: *It is so goddamned easy to drown. It's nothing. One minute you're here, the next minute you're gone. What is life about when it's so fragile? Why do we do such terrible things to each other? Why can't we be so gentle that birds will come and sit on our head, like they do with cows in the fields?*

Just then, as if his thoughts had summoned it, a little brown seabird appeared and alighted on Taso's head. He was astounded. He had just been thinking of that! His hair stood up on end at the coincidence. He rose slowly to his feet and walked into the cabin. There in the mirror he saw the bird, which was attempting to make a sort of nest with his thick black hair.

He went back outside, and his friend saw him. He burst out laughing.

"Look at you!" he said. "That bird must think you're a cow! He's looking for lice!"

Taso didn't speak. He reached up for the bird and held it in his hands. What kind of bird sits for ten or fifteen minutes on someone's head? It was so light, as fragile as life.

He returned down below, with the bird back on his head. After a while, he wanted to lie down. He reached for the bird and looked at it again, and it met his eyes, totally fearless. He opened the door and let it out. It flew around the boat for a while, settling with the sponges before it finally flew off.

As for Taso, it was quite a while before he could fall asleep. He couldn't get that bird out of his mind. And he never has.

21

SURFING WITH DOLPHINS

Dolphins are believed to be the smartest animals on earth—which must be why so many of them make Florida their home. From Panama City to St. Augustine and Clearwater to Miami, marine parks, also known as seaquariums, give visitors an opportunity to watch, feed and even, in places like Theater of the Sea in Islamorada, swim with these magnificent creatures. Of course, they can also be found in the wild, cruising up to eighteen miles an hour or more in warm water ranging from shallow and close to shore to far out to sea. That is, if you're lucky enough to spot them.

There is nothing common about Florida's common bottlenose dolphin, more formally called *Tursiops truncatus*. Growing up to fourteen feet in length and at times surpassing one thousand pounds in weight, these sea mammals can survive and thrive for half a century.

What makes the dolphin such a fan favorite? Maybe it's that adorable upturned mouth, set into a permanent smile. Maybe it's the fact that they are known to form lasting relationships that involve hunting, mating and a whole lot of playing.

Humans are pretty sharp too, of course, and a number of them have figured out how to get a super, and super fun, workout by surfing on a paddle board. Called stand up paddle boarding, stand up paddle surfing or SUP, the sport involves first, a stable board that's ten feet or longer and maybe thirty-one or thirty-two inches wide; second, a paddle; and above all, excellent balance and coordination. (For the uninitiated, traditional paddle boarding

"It's a Copper Whopper!": Water and Weather

Dolphins are believed to be the smartest animals on earth. *Gavin Spencer, freeimages.com.*

involves kneeling or lying on the board while making propulsive swimming movements with the arms.)

I haven't had the pleasure of meeting Carl Fields in person. He told me his story over the phone after having been referred to me by another one of my contributors. That means that I couldn't see his face, but the delight in his voice when he described this experience came through loud and clear. You might find yourself picturing him wearing a big smile when you read this story. Hmmm. Sort of like a dolphin.

FLORIDA WAS THE ONLY place Carl Fields had ever really called home, having moved down with his parents well before his fourth birthday. As a nearly native, he grew up around the water. Even many years later, after he retired, he left his home in Daytona Beach on the Atlantic Coast and rode his bicycle the half mile to the ocean on a regular basis.

This particular early fall morning, he wasn't making the trip alone. Under his arm he carried a paddle and one of his custom-built paddleboards, which he had specially crafted for surfing. Describing his enterprise as part-hobby, part-business, Carl sells his boards for up to $1,000 each. They're special.

Not only are they big enough for surfing—which is becoming ever more popular with paddle boarders—but he also designed these to be used equally well in rivers or lakes, even for fishing.

So there he was, about a mile north of Main Street Pier, around University Beach Approach. The sky shone intensely blue and nearly cloudless, and the water was pristine, with shimmering waves. Not long after Carl had paddled a little way into the surf, he caught sight of a dolphin. He grinned. Not only was it always nice to see a dolphin, but he actually knew this guy.

There's a reason why it's not always hard to recognize a dolphin. Their fins vary quite a lot. Some are curved, others narrow or wide, still others pointed or rounded, even scarred. That's how scientists distinguish one animal from the other when tracking them. But as far as Carl knew, there was only one in the area with a notch in its fin, as though Mother Nature had gone ahead and cut out a hunk of it. He figured he had spotted this guy fifteen or twenty times over the previous couple of years.

Carl enjoyed the cool morning and paddled a while, saw just the right wave and stood up a little straighter on the board. Once more he felt that glorious feeling of riding the surf. There was nothing like it, he reflected, being king of the waves like that. Then, out of the corner of his eye, he noticed that the notched dolphin, *his* dolphin, had caught the same wave. Except it was going in the other direction. It was speeding directly toward him.

It occurred to him, in the next fraction of a second, that this wasn't the first time such a thing had happened to him. He had a vision of a time in Costa Rica, in the seventies, when a much larger dolphin had done the same trick in the Pacific, in stronger waves. Back then he didn't know what was happening, and he remembered having been seriously freaked out, just being there like a sitting duck on his board in the middle of the ocean. Did dolphins attack lone surfers? He didn't think so. But then why did it look so aggressive? Thirty-five years later, he recalled it like it was yesterday. The sea mammal had veered away at the last moment, and all was back to normal—apart from his racing heart.

This time he was older, wiser and, he told himself, as he saw the large creature growing even larger as it approached, he was standing up. That made a lot of difference. He took a single deep breath, which was all he had time for. He checked his stance. And then he waited.

Carl could almost peer deep into the great beast's eyes when the dolphin turned at the last possible moment and dove underwater. He barely had time to be relieved, because he knew that it would probably come back. That's what they usually did. But there he was, alone in the sea with his moment.

He knew there couldn't be anyone else out there, but he couldn't help himself. He looked around in case by some odd chance someone else had materialized out of nowhere to share the experience. He wasn't thinking of a photo or video, nothing like that. Just someone to say, *Yes, that astonishing thing just happened. I will remember it too.* But he was, in fact, completely alone. For the next twenty minutes, he paddled around the area, thinking about how he couldn't believe this had happened to him twice in all the years he'd spent out in the surf.

By this time, the sun was high in the sky. Carl felt his stomach growl and was just considering heading back for shore when the waves parted out toward the horizon, and not one but two shots of gray emerged. Had the big guy come back with his mate? But as they approached, his jaw dropped in surprise. The first dolphin, the one with the notch, was maybe eight or ten feet in length. But the one swimming with it was just a baby. It couldn't have been more than two feet long.

Carl knew just what to do. He crouched on the board, waiting and watching. Then, just as the dolphins started to catch a wave, he rose up and paddled furiously, surfing the same one. This time there were two of them drawing ever nearer to him at top speed, but he held his own. When they veered away at the last second, he watched as they caught up with a third dolphin nearby. This one was just about the same size and truly did look as though it might have been the big guy's mate. He thought he heard them say something to one another before the three of them made their slow way up the coast.

He, on the other hand, would have to return home before he could tell anyone else what had happened. How he had helped teach a baby dolphin that humans can be just like anyone else. Great playmates.

22

WHEN LIGHTNING STRIKES

If Florida ever tires of its nickname the "Sunshine State," it can always change it to the "Lightning Land." That's because although the state ranks fourth (behind Texas, Kansas and Oklahoma) in actual flashes, according to the National Weather Service, it ranks first for lightning *strikes*—and resultant deaths. The reason is simple. There are more of us packed together, and we spend a lot more time outside.

You know the expression, "You have a better chance being struck by lightning?" In Florida, those odds—in a lifetime, that is—aren't too bad: one in three thousand. Oh and by the way, fishing is the number 1 activity that results in lightning deaths. You'll see why that's relevant in a moment.

So why is the Florida peninsula so prone to thunderstorms? It's a simple recipe: mix heat, humidity and sea breezes, then stir. There is good news, however. Overall, thanks to growing public awareness, death by lightning strike is diminishing. Here's a good rule of thumb to keep safe: Take thunderstorms seriously. For every five seconds between a flash of lightning and the roar of thunder, the storm is one mile away. Look for shelter if the storm is six miles away or less.

And just in case you're looking for new vocabulary, here's a term that appears in this story that you may not have ever come across: spoil islands. These are manmade land masses composed of spoil, or waste material dredged up from the construction of navigation channels.

"It's a Copper Whopper!": Water and Weather

Florida ranks first in the nation in lightning strikes—and fatalities. *TJ Smith, freeimages.com.*

Mark Traugott, who kindly told me this story by phone after we were introduced by one of this book's contributors, learned that lesson the hard way, although I strongly suspect he already knew it. This is one of those experiences that another popular expression, "At least you got a good story out of it," was made for.

IT WAS A HOT, humid Saturday morning, even for Florida, and even for summer. But realtor Mark Traugott didn't mind. He had grown up in the state, and he knew that if you wait to do something when it's cool here, particularly in this period of climate change, you'll be waiting a good, long time. Besides, he and his youngest son, Dustin, were going fishing. That meant there'd usually be some kind of breeze on the water to keep things tolerable.

Following his divorce, Mark wasn't able to spend as much time with his kids as he wanted. Every month, he took one or another of the younger ones on a trip like the one they were on that day. They were driving over an hour from the Orlando area to Mosquito Lagoon, between Titusville and Cape Canaveral—not the city, but the actual cape. It's a prime inshore fishing location, blessed with mangroves, sandbars and a mix of both grassy flats and deeper water, the latter due to the presence of spoil islands. It was their special time together, and he knew that Dustin had been looking forward to the day as much as he had.

"I hope we catch us some mangrove snapper," his son said suddenly. The twelve-year-old had already come along with his dad on several of these daylong fishing expeditions, and he was turning into an accomplished angler.

"What about redfish?" Mark asked. "Where we're going is supposed to be the redfish capital of the world. Redfish all year long. Did you know that?"

"That too. And catfish."

"And don't forget sheepshead, with those creepy teeth that look human."

Dustin grinned. "Yeah. Them too." He paused, looked out the window at the passing cars on the highway. "I think we're gonna come back with a good catch today."

"You might be right. Never can tell."

They didn't say much more until they arrived at the lagoon and set down the canoe, a vintage Mohawk two-seater, into the water. Mark gave a few instructions to Dustin, who was helping him load the boat with their tackle boxes, rods and cooler from the car. Then father and son settled down for a relaxing few hours.

"You know we've got some snacks and sodas in the cooler when you're ready," Mark said at one point.

"Yeah, I'm good."

"Not much going on down there today," Dustin muttered, sometime later.

"Nope. Not much."

Morning flowed lazily into afternoon. They were staring into the water so long that they didn't realize that, slowly at first, and then with gathering speed, the sky had begun to turn gray. Mark glanced over to the south and saw that it was even darker in that direction. The wind was starting to pick up, coming from the darkest part of the clouds.

"That's funny," Mark said, rising to his feet. "Looks like a storm brewing, but the wind usually comes out of either the east or west."

Dustin turned to his dad. "Does it matter?"

"Well, it means those big waves are hitting the lagoon from the south. They're already too big for us to paddle to shore. If we don't tie the canoe to that railroad trestle, we could get shot into the open water."

The boy nodded. They'd been in summer storms before, and he knew the drill.

When he was finished, Mark sat back down and watched as the wind whipped the waves around them, causing the canoe to bounce furiously.

"We can ride this one out, right, buddy?"

"It's a Copper Whopper!": Water and Weather

"Sure, Dad."

Then, out of nowhere, it seemed, one of those giant waves crested over the canoe and flooded it. They stood up in the flooded, bouncing canoe and held onto the wood of the railroad trestle.

"Dad! The tackle boxes! They're gone!"

Mark had been so busy he hadn't even noticed. He had put his cellphone in one of the boxes for safe keeping, but he decided not to mention it to Dustin.

"Don't worry. We'll get new ones. We're done fishing for the day, that's for sure. I just want to get us through this storm safe."

They were still floating, but they were stuck, and they knew it. They couldn't untie the boat now, even if they'd wanted to. They'd have to sit this out.

And then a crack of thunder pierced the afternoon sky.

Mark was going to say something comforting, when Dustin cried out, "Dad, look!"

Now what? But when Mark turned around, he let out a shout. To his astonishment, he saw a dazzling white motorboat. The two looked at each other, and Mark knew just what his son was thinking. The craft had come out of nowhere. And the five people onboard looked like angels.

Mark and Dustin waved furiously, but there was no need. The people on the boat had spotted them and were clearly racing toward them to help. It looked to Mark like it was a family. They barely said hello.

"We'll get you aboard, no worries," the father called out to them over the rising wind.

"Thanks," Mark replied. "But I've really got to bring the canoe along. I can't leave it here."

The man looked skeptical, but there was no time for debate. Within minutes, they had tied the canoe to the craft. Mark told Dustin to go with the family; he stayed with the flooded canoe. The strangers towed it over toward a small beach at the east end of the same railroad trestle they had been holding onto. The ride didn't take long, maybe ten minutes, but it was while they were making their way to the beach that it began to pour. Then the lightning lit up the dark sky. It wasn't exactly coming on the heels of the thunder, but it was fierce, nonetheless.

Mark and Dustin looked at each other, their faces grim. When the two crafts reached the beach, the adults on the motorboat unpacked a huge blue tarpaulin, about twenty feet in length. Wordlessly, the two helped them spread it against a two-foot cliff. Then they all crouched down in the sandy dark underneath. Mark and Dustin were on one side; the family—a mother, father and three kids—huddled together on the other.

Now the sky was shooting thunderbolts, and it felt as though they were the targets. In all his years in Florida, Mark had never been through anything like it. Worst of all, the interval between the thunder and lightning was diminishing, and he knew that meant that the lightning was closing in on their location. It got to the point that there was no time at all between the flash of light and the loud bang of the thunder.

That's when it occurred to Mark that this could be the end. At fifty years old, he had never confronted his own death so directly. It hit him with a dull ache, and since he was already on his knees, he put his arm around Dustin and held him tightly. Then he began to pray. It was something he did every week in church, but he had rarely felt such a desperate need as he did at that moment.

"Dear God," he said quietly, "Please save us and save this kind family. We are begging you in our hour of need. Have mercy on us, Lord."

"Oh Lord," Dustin murmured, "Please, please help us! Don't let us die, God! I don't want us to die!"

Once more father and son could read the other's thoughts. Just one year earlier, Dustin's older brother Daniel had died in a traffic accident when the family car was rear-ended. Dustin had been sitting in the front seat.

They hid from the storm maybe a quarter of an hour, and then it started to subside. Cautiously, they all stood up, shook off the tarp and stared out to the lagoon in the direction of the parting storm. All was calm, almost as if it had never happened.

"We can't thank you enough," Mark said to the couple. "You know you saved our lives out there."

"Yeah," Dustin added. "Thanks a lot. Really."

The two shrugged off their gratitude and gathered their family back into their boat. Mark untied the towline. The children waved as they sped away. In a few minutes, they were gone. Father and son then picked up their canoe, turned it upside down to empty it, then plopped it back on top of the shallow water and climbed in. The rest of the trip was, fortunately, uneventful.

Time passed, and Mark took several of his other children out with him fishing that summer. One day, late in the season, he came across an article about a family on a spoil island taking shelter from a thunderstorm. As he looked closer, he saw that the story took place in Mosquito Lagoon, less than ten miles from where he and Dustin had been. The father, he read, was struck by lightning and died.

He felt terrible. But he knew now that it would never happen to him or to his children. He simply wouldn't let it.

23

MUCK IN MY MOCCASINS

Big Cypress Indian Reservation, one of six Seminole reservations in the state, is an eighty-two-thousand-acre parcel of land in the heart of the Everglades. It is home to six hundred descendants of the three-thousand-year-old tribe, known for being the only nation that didn't surrender to the U.S. Army as Native peoples were forced west in the early nineteenth century. In fact, it was the terrain that you will encounter in this story that was in large part responsible for their survival.

Wetlands like the Everglades are best traversed by swamp buggy, a vehicle that can usually move equally well on land, sand, shallow mud and water, and even—although not always—deep mud. As we shall see, however, not all swamp buggies are created equal.

I met Pedro Zepeda, who currently lives in Naples, a couple of years ago through a mutual artist contact. Among many other roles—including educator for the reservation's museum—he is a traditional canoe carver, and his magnificent sixteen-foot indigenous-style canoe was on display that evening. From this connection, I was able to hire him to tell stories at a local library and to work with him on one or two other projects.

Pedro gave me a print of the Everglades that evening, and it hangs in my living room. I pictured the images of that wild, beautiful country as he told me this story.

It was February, the first evening of the Kissimmee Slough Shootout and Rendezvous, and it would be another long day tomorrow. But Pedro Zepeda and his older brother Brian had no intention of calling it quits. They and a small group of volunteers had spent hours in the woods reenacting one

Pedro Zepeda carves traditional Seminole canoes. *Courtesy of Pedro Zepeda.*

of the skirmishes in the Seminole Wars. Like all participants in historical reenactments, they had to don the historic clothing of the period. In their case, it was what Seminoles had worn in the 1830s and 1840s: a plain long shirt, wool or leather leggings, a turban or bandana, vests and moccasins. It was a cool night, but everyone was bundled up warmly in their traditional clothing. Why would anyone want to go home and change back into boring old jackets and sweats?

At the time, the annual event took place at the Ah-Tah-Thi-Ki Museum on Big Cypress Seminole Reservation, where Pedro, who was in his late twenties, worked as a jack-of-all-cultural-trades, from acquisitions board member to oral history coordinator to traditional arts and outreach coordinator. His job entailed educating not only the public but also tribal members about Seminole history. How many people know all there is to know about their heritage?

That night, Pedro and Brian were hanging with Pedro's wife, Kaleena, and six or eight other reenactors from outside the tribe. It was always fun to do these things with outsiders. They enjoyed it too. It felt like they were embodying the culture.

"It always gets me, doing this," one young man said suddenly. "Ever since you said what you did that time about the Seminole wars, Pedro."

Pedro had been talking to Kaleena; now he looked up. "What? What did I say?"

"The whole thing about the three Seminole wars with the U.S. I mean really; wasn't it just one big one, from 1817 to 1858?"

"Oh yeah, that's right. The U.S. soldiers could go home, take a break, say their job was done for the moment. But not us. We didn't get any breaks. We were just stuck in it."

"It's a Copper Whopper!": Water and Weather

Brian yawned. They'd been talking about killing all day, one way or another. He was ready for a break.

"So, what do you want to do now?" he asked the group. "Unless you want to call it a night?"

"No way," one of the volunteers said. "We're up for anything!"

"We haven't seen much of the woods," her husband pointed out. "That would be cool."

Brian rose to his feet. "That's an idea. It's a great night, and this time of year, the ground is in good shape. Let's do a swamp buggy ride. We'll show you the old cypress trees. And the marsh." The brothers often took people out on swamp buggies, and it was always a popular activity.

Brian left for a few minutes to get the museum's swamp buggy. He owned a few himself, but this one was a monster, with five- or six-foot tires. It was articulated in the middle, which made it easier to maneuver. Pedro, meanwhile, picked up the keys for a smaller one, which the reservation had purchased for its short-lived Motocross track.

Swamp buggies are loud. Maybe not as loud as airboats, but loud. So the occupants of the two vehicles made their way toward the woods without much conversation, but with plenty of laughing. Every time they passed over the limestone outcroppings in their path, the passengers—especially those standing up and leaning on the railing in Brian's buggy—jumped a mile. In fact, the brothers called one of the roads they drove on "Kidney Shaker Road" for just that reason.

Pedro followed beyond Brian. His brother was quite a bit older, and Pedro had always looked up to him. This was the man who had taught him to carve canoes. More to the point, this was the man who owned his own swamp buggies. Pedro trusted his brother more than almost anyone else he knew.

They were passing over the dirt roads at a good clip when they took a left, then turned right into a marsh. What of it? That's what the swamp buggies were for. Everyone was in high spirits when all at once Pedro's vehicle got stuck. It had sunk into the muck of the marsh. Brian, meanwhile, had stopped some distance ahead.

"Didn't you hear me?" he called out.

"How was I supposed to hear you?" Pedro asked with a frown. "I can't hear anything when those engines are going."

"Well I yelled at the top of my lungs, but I also tried to wave you back."

The passengers in Pedro's vehicle were silent. He considered for a moment. Then he asked, "You stuck too?"

"No, of course not. But I could see how mushy it was getting. I didn't think you could make it on that puny little thing."

Pedro nodded slowly. "You got that right." He leaned over the side. In the glow of his headlights, he could see just how bad the situation was.

"Damn. I'm stuck up to the axle. We must be two feet deep."

"Well," said his brother, "let's get to work. Try to spin your wheels a little more."

"I did it plenty. It's no use." Still, he put the motor in gear and hit the gas. The tires spun helplessly. It was then that Pedro heard a *thump, thump, thump, thump*. Now what? And then, out of the sky like filthy hail, chunks of mud poured down on his head. Frantically, he tried to flap it away.

"What the hell was *that*?"

The rest of the group started to howl with glee. Finally, Brian said, "It was from your tires. The mud was flying thirty feet up in the air and then raining back down on you!"

When the laughter died down, one of the volunteers asked, "Are we going to get out?" There was a hint of anxiety in her voice.

"Of course!" Pedro assured her. "No sweat. It'll just take a while. First thing, everybody's got to get off. We have to lighten the load."

And one by one, they climbed out of the dune buggy into the mud. They sank down way past their moccasins and halfway up their leggings. Meanwhile the lucky onlookers on Brian's vehicle leaned along the waist-high railing, enjoying the spectacle.

"Oh gross!" someone called out. "I'm glad I don't have to do your wash tomorrow!"

Once everyone was out, Pedro climbed back in and again tried to force the tires out of the muck. But if anything, they were sinking lower.

"Do you have any shovels?" one of Pedro's passengers asked.

"Nah, but I do have a chain. Brian! Let's hook these two buggies together, and you can pull me out."

It took two tries, and close to an hour, but at last, the brothers were able to hook the back of Brian's swamp buggy to Pedro's front bumper, and Brian towed him out of the mud and onto drier land. Then everybody clambered back into the vehicles and made their way home, happy and filthy.

"It's a good thing our ancestors didn't have swamp buggies," Pedro said to Kaleena later that night. "We might've lost the war."

"You're right," she said quietly. "Seeing the way the mud was our enemy tonight, I'm glad it was our friend back then. Almost makes me sorry for the soldiers."

"M-mmm." He was listening, but he was also thinking what an educational ending this had been to an educational day. It's one thing to teach something, he reflected. It's quite another to live it.

Part 3

"A *GALLO* IN MIAMI?"

FAUNA AND FLORA

24

THE LAST *GRINGO* IN HIALEAH

Q: What do Amelia Earhart, Fidel Castro and J.P. Morgan have in common?

A: They all left their marks on Hialeah, Florida.

Located half an hour northwest of Miami, the city of Hialeah—"high prairie," in the Seminole language—is one of the largest in the state. For a long time, it was best known for the historic Hialeah Park Race Track, which opened in 1922 and entertained the likes of Winston Churchill, Harry Truman and J.P. Morgan. It was also where the vanished aviator Earhart took off from on her last, ill-fated flight in 1937. And since the Cuban Revolution in 1959, it has become the U.S. city with the highest concentration of Cubans and Cuban Americans—over 73 percent—and is widely considered a rousing immigrant success story.

Lucia Gonzalez, my source for the following tale, is not only director of the North Miami Public Library but also an acclaimed storyteller and children's book author. In fact, her book *The Bossy Gallito*, like this one, a story about a rooster, was awarded the Pura Belpré Children's Literature Honor Medal and was included in the New York Public Library's list of 100 Picture Books Everyone Should Know. Having arrived in Miami at age fourteen, hers can be considered a rousing immigrant success.

I have known Lucia for several years as a fellow storyteller, and I have hired her to perform both for college students and for the general public. In addition to her tales, her warmth and naturalness make her an audience favorite.

In Cuba, the rooster is a symbol of strength and power. *Esther Groen, freeimages.com.*

Lucia's father Pepe was a *campesino*, a tobacco farmer in rural Camito del Guayabal. He loved Cuba; he loved his family; he loved his life. When Fidel Castro came to power, however, he and his wife and two daughters escaped to Miami along with many other anti-Communist refugees. He was forty-two years old, and he found himself doing what for him would have not so long before been unheard of: starting a new chapter in a new country.

"A *Gallo* in Miami?": Fauna and Flora

Pepe was lucky. He soon found work as a cook in an upscale Italian restaurant called Marcella's. He fit right in. In fact, he learned Italian before he learned English. His family had enough to eat, and he had a steady, if small, paycheck.

His biggest complaint was that his boss didn't want him to smoke his fat Cuban cigars in the kitchen. One day she saw him stirring a pot with the cigar between his teeth and yelled, "Per Dio! For God sakes!" Pepe understood her Italian and English words in Spanish, however, to mean "Get lost; you're no good!" He was horribly insulted until the linguistic miscommunication was smoothed out.

His *other* biggest complaint: apartment living. He felt trapped without the land he used to see outside his front door. Above all, Pepe wanted a fenced-in yard. So he hit on a plan. He saved every dollar he could so that the family would be able, one day, to move to a real house. After three years, when he had finally accumulated enough cash, he plunked down a security deposit on a five-room rental property in Hialeah. He became a gardener, both professionally and after hours. And he had a fenced-in yard at last.

But the yard wasn't for a family dog. Now that he had a little land, the thing Pepe missed most about Cuba, apart from the family he'd left behind, was being awakened at dawn by a rooster. And so he set out to buy one.

"Pepe," said his wife when he brought home his feathered purchase, "are you *loco*? A *gallo* in Miami? What are you thinking?"

"I'm thinking that everyone around us is from Cuba or somewhere else where they wake up to roosters. I'm thinking the neighbors will thank me for reminding them of their homeland. Not to mention for waking them up with the sun. And if they don't, who cares? I'll be happy. This is my home, and a rooster is all I need to make this a true paradise."

"I still think you're *loco*," she said. But she didn't say anything more about it. At least not for a while. For the first three mornings, the rooster woke up the family, and the neighborhood, with the dawn. Every country's roosters speak a different language, of course. In Cuba, they say, "Ki-ki-ri-ki."

The rooster's crowing was not the signal for the family to get out of bed. It was still far too early. It was just the time when Pepe opened his eyes, felt right at home, smiled and either went back to sleep or didn't. He was a free man, after all, and this was a free country.

But that third morning, not long after dawn, there was an officious-sounding knock on the front door. Pepe jumped out of bed, pulled on a shirt and opened up. His wife was close behind him, still in her bathrobe. To their shock, they faced a lanky, mustachioed, uniformed member of Hialeah's Finest.

Pepe, who didn't speak English, had no idea what was happening. But his wife understood immediately, even if she didn't know the words.

"It's the *gallo*," she murmured to her husband in Spanish, while the policeman continued to talk. "I told you it was a bad idea. I'll bet somebody complained."

Her husband turned to her. "Who would complain?" he asked. "Why would anyone complain? Go get Lucia."

Seventeen-year-old Lucia was used to being summoned to interpret for her parents. In fact, she was up and dressed before she even heard her name called.

"May I help you, officer?" she asked.

"There's been a complaint," he said, obviously relieved to find an English speaker in the house. "Your neighbor. He's been awakened three mornings in a row by your rooster. I understand how you people like your poultry," he said with a grin. "But this is a neighborhood, not a farm. People gotta get their sleep."

"Of course," Lucia said, nodding. "Let me just explain that to my dad." She wasn't looking forward to the task. It wasn't just that her father would be upset. It was that she had already come to love the little rooster herself. She too had awakened and smiled in the half-light when he crowed. She too missed home.

When she finished explaining the situation to her father, he was indignant. "Tell me," he asked the patrolman in Spanish, "who was it that complained?" Lucia dutifully translated.

The young man hesitated. "Well, we usually don't say, but it's the older man and his wife two doors down." He cocked his head to the left.

Lucia had barely gotten the words out to her father when he spat out, "I knew it! It's the *gringo*! *El Americano*! He is always so sneaky. Always watching us. Waiting for us to trip up."

The officer stayed in the house just long enough for Lucia to assure him that the rooster would go. That very day. After he left, her father could barely contain his fury.

He did get rid of the rooster, of course. He had no choice. He couldn't bring himself to butcher it himself, but the family enjoyed *arroz con pollo*, rooster soup and any number of other delicacies for days to come.

It took quite a while for Lucia and her siblings to overcome the impression of *gringos* as sneaky and that, in fact, a hardworking man had just wanted to get some sleep. And to his dying day, when her father told the story, he would always end by saying, "Who would have thought that we would have the luck to find the last *gringo* in Hialeah?"

25
AUNT MINNIE MAE GETS SUPPER

No collection of Florida stories would be complete without an entry from the Keys. Best known for the flashy Key West of Ernest Hemingway and Mallory Square at sunset, the Keys are all that and so much more. Extending more than 120 miles into the Florida Straits between the Atlantic Ocean from the Gulf of Mexico, they lure tourists with a yen for boating, snorkeling, diving and, of course, fishing.

And just in case you're wondering, a key, or quay, or cay is a naturally occurring low island, like a coral reef or sandbar. The archipelago known as the Florida Keys is made of coral, and the city of Marathon, where this story takes place, is spread across thirteen islands in all.

Sheldon Voss is a fourth-generation Floridian on his father's side, tracing his ancestry back to the Pierces, who arrived from Chicago in the late 1800s, and the Vosses (third generation) from Maine a little later. This is one of many Florida memories he likes to share.

Beginning in the late 1950s, Sheldon's dad was a charter boat fisherman out of Bahia Mar, in Fort Lauderdale. He and his boat the *Lucky Lady* did a good business hosting parties, company outings and other gatherings. Sure, he had to buy his own fuel and drinks for the guests. But he would also arrange for a photographer to come snap photos of the fishing party and the catch—and get a commission (read: kickback) from the guy. He would arrange for the taxidermist to mount the fish and receive another few dollars. In an era before any kind of serious health inspection, he would also fillet and weigh the fish the clients didn't take with them and wrap it up and sell it

Aunt Minnie Mae is in front, wearing the checked shirt. Sheldon Voss is the one drinking, with his father's assistance. *Courtesy of Sheldon Voss.*

from the dock, leaving the carcasses behind. Life wasn't necessarily easy, but it was sweet—and fairly profitable.

By the early 1960s, however, the business was changing. People with the means and interest began to purchase fifty-foot yachts—so-called fishing machines—and, because they didn't know how to maintain or operate them, they'd hire a captain, like Sheldon's dad, to take them to tournaments up and down the coast. One such couple kept their boat docked at a house in Marathon Shores, near Vaca Cut, just down the canal from the Vosses' Keys home.

Sheldon's mother rarely accompanied her husband on these trips, but this time the tournaments were in Nassau and Bimini, and she decided to go along for the ride. Because it was summer, it would be no problem for little Shelly, age ten, to leave home as well. It was arranged that he would stay at the house with his aunt Minnie Mae, who lived just north of Lauderdale in Pompano, along with her sister Annie Jane and grandson Dusty.

"A *Gallo* in Miami?": Fauna and Flora

Aunt Minnie Mae had come to Florida by way of Georgia. With her buttery southern drawl, ever-present highball glass and cigarette dangling from her lips, she was a memorable character for her nephew. He was looking forward to having the company, especially Dusty, who was his own age. And he was looking forward to going to the Marathon house even more. A dock out the back door! He'd been fishing since forever, but this was something really special. He couldn't wait.

It was mid-September 1960, and Hurricane Donna had recently battered the Keys, along with Cuba, the Bahamas and, in a weakened state, a large swath of the East Coast. In the Keys, it was the worst hurricane in twenty-five years. On the ride down with his mother in a Greyhound bus, Sheldon saw smashed roofs flung hundreds of yards from buildings, houses ripped from their foundations and all manner of uprooted trees. He had no idea that this was unusual. As far as he was concerned, his parents had bought a house on the moon.

But when he got down there and walked through the front door, into the kitchen and out the back to the dock, he immediately felt at home. Spread before his eyes were the ocean, the flats and Key Colony Beach. A fisherman's dream!

The first few days after his mother left were Shelly Voss's idea of heaven. When they weren't at the beach or fishing, Minnie would treat them to her wonderful southern cooking. Shelly particularly adored her potato salad, which for the rest of his life he would remember fondly. Minnie was having a grand ol' time herself, drinking and visiting with Annie Jane.

One early evening, Minnie Mae stood up, took a long drag off her cigarette and announced to the group that she was fixing to cook dinner.

"Annie Jane can help with the side dishes," she said. "Shelly, Dusty, all I need from you young 'uns is to go on back and catch us a big ol' fish."

"Yes, ma'am!" they answered in unison.

Shelly and Dusty had come prepared. They picked up their state-of-the-art fishing tackle, lures, hook and bobbers. Over the last few days, they'd caught skipjack and regular jackfish and a tiny silvery fish commonly called look-downs, which Mrs. Voss always called moonfish, because they reflected the light. They sat down at the dock with paraphernalia in hand and—nothing. No worries. They changed bait from shrimp to ballyhoo and back again, all of which they'd grabbed from Shelly's dad's freezer. They changed lures; they changed everything they could think of. But, incredibly, no luck. Every once in a while, they'd meet each other's eyes in disbelief. How could they go back inside without the main course? Why were the fish not biting? What were they doing wrong?

They hadn't said a word or made a sound for close to half an hour. So they jumped when the kitchen door leading out to the dock suddenly flew open as if it had been kicked by a gunfighter. The first thing they saw was a puff of smoke. This was soon followed by Minnie, her glass half-full (or half-empty, depending on how you looked at it) with honey-colored Southern Comfort.

Without saying a word, she set the glass on a piling, reached around the corner of the house and pulled out a plain old cane pole that neither boy had known was there.

"You boys not having any luck, huh?" she asked, her voice warm and sympathetic.

In unison, they answered, "No, ma'am."

To this day, Sheldon doesn't know what she used to bait the hook. Maybe it was bacon from the kitchen. In any case, she let fly in the exact same spot where the boys had been. And faster than you could say "Come and get it," she was reeling in dinner.

It was a huge snapper, maybe two feet in length. Calm as could be, she unhooked the flopping fish at the little table that sat on the dock for just this purpose. Then she reached into the back pocket of her jeans, stabbed the fish, scaled it, flipped it over, finished the job and tossed the carcass—all in a manner of a few minutes.

She hadn't looked at the boys since she'd cast off. Now she turned to them, fish in hand, and said the two words they'd been waiting for.

"Let's eat!"

The fish was more than enough for the four of them. It tasted out of this world. Almost, Sheldon recalls, as good as the potato salad.

26

PELICAN URGENT CARE

The Boca Inlet in Boca Raton connects the Intracoastal Waterway to the Atlantic Ocean. For sailors, it's located at ICW Mile 1048. For the rest of us landlubbers, it sits on Ocean Boulevard, aka State Road A1A, along the beach. South Inlet Park boasts a kiddie playground, picnic tables and barbeque pits.

That's the setting of this story—now, for the characters. Florida boasts two types of pelican: the brown, which lives here year-round; and the "snowbird" white pelican, which migrates south for the winter. "Snowbird" doesn't only refer to a bird, of course. That's the term Floridians use to describe the northerners who come for the season, either to rent or to occupy the real estate they leave vacant during the rest of the year. The human variety is in far greater abundance here than the avian, to be sure. It also spends considerably more time and money at the local flea markets.

Of the two types of pelican, the brown is the more common. It's easy to spot waddling on piers or boat docks, posing on concrete pilings—or diving headfirst into the water, only to emerge with that fish you were hoping to catch yourself.

The story features a few human characters as well. I've known Lori and Joel Vinikoor for twenty years. A dear friend, Lori was one of my first victims—I mean volunteers—for the public radio segment. But this isn't just one of the first stories I recorded for the Public Storyteller. It's also one of my all-time favorites. Doctors performing surgery on a bird on a Florida pier? It doesn't get any better than that.

The brown pelican is the most common in Florida. *Elvis Santana, freeimages.com.*

LORI AND JOEL VINIKOOR are retired podiatrists who moved to South Florida from New Jersey. One brisk winter day not long after their arrival, they paid a visit to Lori's sister and brother-in-law, who live in a luxury condo on the ocean, quite close to the pier at the Boca Inlet. The couple arrived early, so they decided to take a walk from the condo where they had parked their car down to the inlet. They picked their way through stones and boulders out to the very end, where they watched the sparkling boats sailing in and out, some one-person crafts, others magnificent yachts.

After a while, the two decided to set out walking the pier. People fish on it all the time, whether for tarpon, mangrove snapper or any number of species of saltwater fish. There didn't seem to be good-sized fish snapping at the bait, but the families and lone fishermen did appear to be having a good time, sitting in the sun with their pails, tackle boxes and poles—not to mention the occasional beer or sandwich.

The couple leaned on the worn wooden railing and watched the action for a while. Before long, the human fishermen were joined by nonhuman competition—brown pelicans. The pelicans didn't seem to be after fish, however, since so few were biting. Instead, they were trying to grab hold of the bait.

"Look at that guy over there," Joel said, tapping Lori on the shoulder. "He's trying to cast his line, but the pelican won't let him. Maybe he's jealous."

"He's going to get hurt if he's not careful," Lori replied.

"Who, the fisherman?"

"The pelican. Those hooks are sharp!"

Meanwhile, the men and women on the pier were starting to grumble about the birds. Some of them clapped or yelled to get them out of the way, but few of the creatures actually felt the need to leave. The pelican that was bothering the young man closest to them certainly wasn't going anywhere anytime soon.

All at once, the fisherman let out a yelp. Or maybe it was the pelican. Just as Lori had predicted, the man had hooked the bird, whose brown feathers were now ruffled in an odd way. As the two doctors approached for a closer look, they saw to their horror that the hook wasn't just in the animal's mouth. It had lodged about an inch below the eye, and maybe the same distance above the bill.

Four or five fishermen jumped forward to see what they could do to remove the hook. But when they saw the damage, they stood back again.

"There are barbs on those hooks," Joel murmured.

"I know," Lori said, nodding. "What a mess." She winced. "Joel, we've got to do something! If they try to take it out, they're going to torture that poor bird!" As a matter of fact, at that very moment someone had come forward to pull at the hook.

"Stop it!" Joel called. "You'll pull out a piece of its brain along with the hook!"

"Excuse me," Lori said, pushing her way forward. She wasn't sure the men spoke English, but by then, a small crowd was gathering on the pier, and she figured someone would.

"We're doctors," she said, looking around at the curious faces. "We do surgery. We can help. Without killing the pelican."

The crowd took several steps back, as if on cue. Lori and Joel knelt down beside the bird, whose good eye looked frantic. Lori grabbed the pelican's beak. She was surprised how easy it was to hold. The bird didn't seem to be able to open it much once she did.

"It's as soft as velvet," she said in surprise, to no one in particular. The beak was quite long but didn't seem to be very strong. Cartilage and bone covered with skin, she figured.

She held the beak down while Joel attempted to pull out the hook. It wasn't coming out though, due to the lethal barb.

"Does anyone have any wire-cutters?" Joel asked.

Out of the crowd, an older man produced wire-cutters with a hook remover. Joel nodded his thanks. Then the two doctors set to work, attempting to cut the fish hook without hurting the flesh.

When they had finished, they gently pulled the hook from one side to the other. To their surprise, there was hardly any blood. The patient lay perfectly motionless until Lori let him go. The bird took one grateful look at the pair, she was sure. And then it flew away.

"Nice work, doctor," Lori said, rising to her feet with a smile.

"Thank you, doctor," Joel replied.

It took them longer than they'd expected to get off the pier and onto the road. Everyone they passed wanted to shake hands, to congratulate them on their work. To the Vinikoors, however, it was no big deal. You might say it's like being a marine. Once a doctor, always a doctor. Even if the patient is a pelican.

27
IN DOG WE TRUST

I wish I could say that the catalyzing event of this story is truly an "only in Florida" occurrence, but it has become all too familiar in communities across the country. Still, I knew I had to include it here, if only for the particular message of hope that this tale brings.

Columbine. Sandy Hook. Virginia Tech. The list of schools assailed by gun violence is long and, horribly, growing longer with each passing year. When Marjory Stoneman Douglas (MSD) High School in tony Parkland, Florida, was added to that list in 2018, students and parents raised their voices, like others before them, to say, "No more." But, of course, there have been more.

Apart from the fact that every story is unique, the aftermath of the MSD tragedy did inspire some extraordinary transformation, particularly among its survivors. Grace Briden's story is one small part of it.

I met Grace through the Parkland Library, where she had provided support to victims and families of the shooting. As we sat outside a nearby coffee shop, I could tell right away that she wasn't your typical teenager. The poise and thoughtfulness with which she shared her story told me that she would have gone far even had she not grown as a result of this tragedy.

GRACE BRIDEN WAS A fifteen-year-old high school junior on February 14, 2018. Like some of her classmates, she had spent much of the school day thinking about an upcoming test in biology (phylum, class, order, family, genus, species). But for Grace, it was particularly hard to concentrate, in part because she

Grace Briden's dog Duncan has his own ID card. *Courtesy of Grace Briden.*

had no Valentine close by. Having lived nearly all her life overseas until half a year earlier, Grace missed her best friends, who were thousands of miles away. In her spare moments throughout the day, she read and responded to their loving posts ("You're my Valentine!") on Facebook.

During the test, there was a fire drill. So when the alarm sounded during the last twenty minutes of Spanish, her final class of the day, Grace and those around her figured it was just another drill and they could go home early. She was more than ready. Quickly, she gathered her books and exited the classroom.

But once outside class, Grace heard several teachers scream, "Get back in your rooms! Get out of the hall! Lock the doors!"

She turned back, but the door to the room was already locked. Confused and anxious, she looked around and caught the eye of another teacher, who motioned to her to come into her classroom. Inside, the students were huddled into a corner around a uniformed security guard with a crackling two-way radio.

It was then that the gunshots coming through the radio registered on her consciousness. Were they blanks? Was this another drill? It was only at the unmistakable thrum of helicopters that some of the students started to cry.

When Grace and her classmates emerged from the room four hours later, seventeen people were dead.

After the shooting, the school was closed for two weeks. Students and faculty mourned the victims and dealt with the trauma as best they could. Grace's parents engaged a psychotherapist for her almost immediately, and she continued to attend sessions for months.

The first thing Grace remembers seeing on her return to school was a goat. Despite her anxiety, she smiled. Therapy goats are, of course, not as common as therapy dogs, but those were in the school, too. The word was put out that any student was allowed to spend as much time as he or she wished in the lunchroom with human or four-legged therapists, or both.

"A *Gallo* in Miami?": Fauna and Flora

The moment Grace encountered Lori Bale, the human member of a therapy team with a dog named Daisy, she knew the woman had nothing but love in her heart. Whether it was her smile, her easy manner or something else, Grace found Lori especially nice, and unlike her impression of some of the other helpers, didn't seem to be doing this just to get her name in the news or to have a good story to tell.

"So, how's your day been so far?" she asked Grace that first day. The two talked about Daisy. In fact, it wasn't until maybe a month after the shooting that they discussed the events of that terrible day. Until then, they just talked. About what, she couldn't say. About whatever she needed to talk about.

"I've spent all my life out of the country," Grace said one day. "I was born in Michigan, but we lived most recently in Ghana, and before that Kuwait, Mali and Chile, because my dad has been a doctor for embassies all over the world."

It was sometime in March that Grace turned to Lori with a pointed question.

"Do you think I could do this with my dog?" she asked, pointing to Daisy as casually as she could.

Lori cocked her head. "What's your dog like?"

"Oh, Duncan's eight. He's my second dog, actually. He was in Ghana with me. He's always been such a chill, happy dog. He doesn't play with toys, and he never ever bites."

"Why do you want to do this?" the woman asked.

"Well, I want to be a nurse someday, and I never had the opportunity to do this kind of thing when I lived overseas. You see, I didn't even know this kind of thing existed."

The next time she saw her, Lori gave Grace all the information for the test she would have to take to get Therapy Dog International (TDI) certification.

The actual training took Grace by surprise. She had raised Duncan from a puppy. He already knew sit, stay, come, down and drop it.

"It's funny," she told Lori a week or so later. "We've been reinforcing all those things, no problem. But 'leave it'? Now that's *hard* for him."

"You know what they say about old dogs and new tricks," Lori observed.

Grace worked with Lori for a month, going over what she and Duncan would need to do for the test. Then she trained alone with Duncan for another three months. She and the twenty-three-pound Cairn terrier worked outside together every day.

In May, just three months after the shooting, they passed the certification test with points to spare. And then, all at once, it was the last day of school, the day that Grace had planned to take Duncan on his first assignment.

That morning, Duncan woke her up early, as if he were ready to work. The night before, Grace had barely slept. She put on her special red TDI shirt, and Duncan wore his official bandana.

Grace and Lori signed in at the school office along with a few other dog teams. When her friends saw Duncan, they crowded around the two. She passed out Duncan's new TDI cards, which explained what he liked and didn't like. (Tugging his tail was okay, and he was used to wheelchairs from the time in fourth grade that Grace had been injured.)

Then her friends went their separate ways. Grace was just settling in her seat when one student she didn't really know came up and started talking to Duncan, never looking Grace in the eye.

"I like your hair," the young girl told him. "Just like my dog. Do you have a card?"

Duncan panted happily, while Grace handed the girl Duncan's card with a smile. She didn't mind that the girl talked only to Duncan, far from it. She knew what it was to be shy and alone from having changed schools so often.

The bell rang to signal the end of the school day, but still the girl didn't move. She just kept tickling Duncan behind his ears and rubbing his belly. After she had been sitting about half an hour, she sighed and rose to leave.

"I just lost my dog," she said suddenly, her eyes still on the terrier. "And—a couple of friends. I don't know how I'm going to make it this summer. It's just so hard. You really made my day."

Grace nodded. There was nothing to say. Duncan had said it all.

28
THE KITE WHISPERER

Rodney Welch is that rare older Floridian: a native. Next to Arizona, Florida has the second-smallest percentage of native-born residents of all fifty states. And of those, a good number are quite young. It makes sense. Not only has the state been a retirement haven for some time, but sitting as it does just ninety miles from Havana, it is also an oasis of freedom for Cubans, Haitians and Venezuelans, among others. And let's not forget those spring breakers who fell in love with the sand and sun.

We mustn't forget northern professionals, either. With no state tax, relatively low property taxes and mile upon mile of gorgeous coastline and waterways, many people who could get great jobs—and lousy commutes—elsewhere in the country are drawn to the Florida lifestyle. This story may make them think twice before sampling the local flora, however. At least with their bare skin.

The setting is Lauderdale by the Sea, a narrow strip of barrier island set between the Atlantic Ocean and the manmade Intracoastal Waterway. The town is about 1.5 square miles in size, with less than a mile of that on dry land. Because the island is a popular spot for scuba diving, its main industry is, you guessed it, tourism.

There are actually three main characters in this story, if you count the villain. Coconut palms grow wild from Jupiter to Key West on the state's east coast and from Sarasota to Marco Island on the west. They are also cultivated as far north as Cocoa Beach and Clearwater.

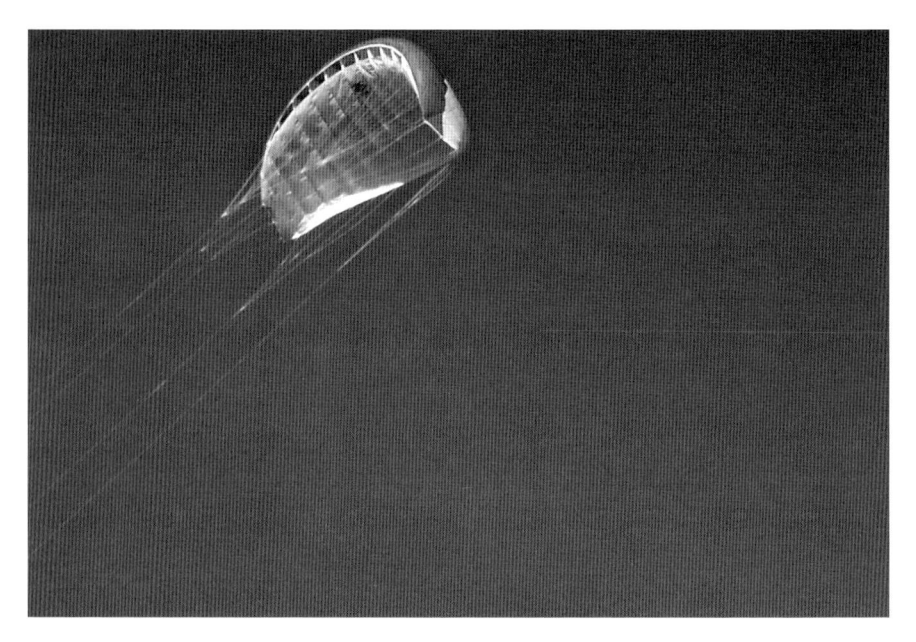

Florida coastal breezes make Fort Lauderdale a perfect location for flying kites. *Ruth Semple, freeimages.com.*

Rodney, however, was born in Miami and spent his later childhood in Melbourne Beach. He says that where he grew up, there were no coconut palms. But there was NASA. Which accounts for the bravery. And maybe also the tolerance of heights.

When Rodney Welch moved back to South Florida after spending decades in other parts of the state, he stayed for a while in his sister's house in Fort Lauderdale. He had been gone so long that he didn't know many people. Plus, he needed a job. His sister had a lot of contacts, and he hoped to make the most of them.

After just a few days, his sister suggested an outing. A friend of hers was having a party, and she wanted to bring Rodney along. The hostess was nice enough, and he was glad to meet her and some of his sister's other friends.

About a week later, Rodney had found himself his own little apartment. It was the weekend of the annual boat show in Fort Lauderdale, and he was riding his bicycle home when he decided to drop in to say hi to his sister. The woman who had thrown the party the week before was sitting on the deck when he arrived.

They got to talking, and he mentioned that he was looking for work.

"Do you happen to know anything about the sign business?" she asked.

"Sure. I'm pretty familiar with it from some of the jobs I've had in the past."

"Well," she said, "my ex-husband owns the biggest sign shop in the county, and I'm pretty sure he's looking for help. Hold on. Let me check."

And then and there, she reached in her bag for her phone, made a quick call and, on hanging up, announced that Rodney should appear Monday for an interview in the sign shop's art department.

Rodney got the job. To show his gratitude, he called the woman and asked her out to dinner.

"Tell you what," she said. "Why don't you go to the supermarket and get us some steaks and a bottle of wine. We can eat at my house. I'll make the side dishes."

That sounded good to Rodney. He picked up the food, and then he picked up a map. Since the woman lived near Lauderdale by the Sea, he checked out the beach behind the Aruba Beach Café on the north side of the pier. It looked like a great place for kite-flying, and the wind, he figured, would be just about right. Then he selected a kite, one of nearly fifty in the collection he'd amassed over the years. It was a stunt kite, a Lotus, six feet wide, with an orange, red and black pattern. The Lotus is known to be fast and active, meaning it tends to be easy to fly.

It was, he knew, also a great way to break the ice on a first date. He'd done it before. Stand behind the woman, raise your arms so she can lay hers on yours like she's holding a set of handlebars, then gradually let her hold the strings, all the while letting the wind yank you up against her. It was better than dancing.

He showed up at his date's door at six o'clock, dressed in shorts, a flowery Hawaiian shirt and tennis shoes. They had a drink, grilled and ate the steaks and sides and, then, since it was October, and the days not as long as in the height of summer, quickly left the house for the beach.

The Aruba Beach Café is set against about one hundred feet of beachfront, which that night was alive with the swaying of dozens of coconut palms. It's a popular hangout for tourists and locals to eat, drink, listen to music and dance. The night they were there, the wind blew strong out of the northeast. Maybe 150 people filled the glass-encased bar. The moon had risen, and the kite was soon prancing through the air, with Rodney and his date watching it from the ground, standing close.

All was going well for the two kite flyers—that is, until it wasn't. Before they knew what was happening, the wind blew the pair too close to the coconut palms, and the kite nose-dived into the fifteen-foot fronds atop the tree. Rodney tried to finesse the strings. He did all the tricks he'd learned over the years, but to no avail. The epitome of bird-like freedom just a few moments before was now hopelessly treed. After several tries, Rodney threw the kite strings onto the sand and leaned against the rough tree trunk, looking up at the sky.

"What are you doing?" the woman asked.

"I've tried everything. I'm licked. Let's just forget it and sit here and watch the moon rise."

"But your kite!"

"Trust me; it won't stay up there forever. Someday the wind will loosen it, a kid will find it and it will make his day."

She was silent a full minute. Then her eyes lit up. "Hey, I have a friend. He's an electrician. He's got a ladder tall enough to get it down." She reached for her phone. "I'll call him."

Rodney shook his head. "It's just a kite! I've got dozens of them! Forget it!"

Maybe it was her nervousness on a first date. Maybe it was her guilt at not flying the kite well enough. But she wouldn't take no for an answer.

"I'm telling you; he lives nearby. He won't mind at all. He's a great guy."

Visions of a faceless, muscle-bound electrician hero filled Rodney's head. Not much of a way for him to make an impression on a date. "It's fine, really."

"I can't let you leave it like this."

Ultimately, when faced with the prospect of the electrician, neither could Rodney. Without saying a word, he kicked off his tennis shoes and, using his inner thighs, shins and arms, proceeded to shimmy up the coconut tree. Now this wasn't Rodney's first rodeo or, rather, tree-climbing expedition. Born in what was then called Dade County (now Miami-Dade), he had climbed the local pine trees in wild, natural areas brimming with palmetto and scrub. He had even climbed dwarf coconut trees, or tall ones that grew at an angle, pitched low to the ground. He had always been agile and athletic. Of course, that was when he was seven. Now he was forty-seven.

The tree was easily thirty feet high, but it didn't take him long to reach the top. Once there, he grabbed one of the lower fronds, reached for the kite with his other hand and worked at loosening it, all the while tightly squeezing the trunk with his legs. After a few minutes he was able to shake the kite free and let it drop to the ground.

Paying close attention to his movements, he lifted the free arm that had dropped the kite and wrapped it around the trunk. He took the other arm and did the same, releasing the pressure just a little so he could ease himself down. But the trunk was only about eight inches in diameter, making it tough to grip. All at once he felt himself slide, about ten feet down the tree.

This would have been an uncomfortable sensation on any tree when wearing shorts, but a coconut palm is not just any tree. Its trunk is covered with fine, hair-like fibers. These hairs caught in Rodney's skin as he slid down. It all happened very fast. When he finally made it to the sand, he looked at his arms. The tender skin was shredded and filled with those nasty fibers. It burned, itched and throbbed, all at the same time. Meanwhile, the same thing was happening on the inside of his thighs and shins. Even the tops of his bare feet were skinned and burning. To add to the scene, blood from the abrasions dripped down his extremities.

He was, to put it simply, in agony.

His date looked at him and said, "My God."

But that's not the end of the story. All at once, they noticed a commotion from inside the Aruba. They hadn't realized that they were standing directly in the rays of a floodlight. They might as well have been on stage. Their audience: the hundred-plus patrons of the café. Apparently, everyone had watched Rodney's heroic climb and his ignominious fall. Now they were applauding and cheering so loudly that they were audible through the glass and over the roar of the ocean.

The two on the beach looked at the crowd in shock. At least Rodney was in shock. Any bit of cognition on his part was directed to the pain and the fact that he would have scars on his body for years. His date, however, was thinking of the nearer future.

"Hey," she said, her eyes wide. "Look at that! We should go inside. I bet they'll give us a free drink!"

They're not still together.

29

HER FIRST CRAB

Merritt Island in Brevard County is not an island. It's a peninsula. That fact is totally inconsequential to this little tale, but since it's about a surprise catch, it seems only fitting to start it off with a surprise. The landmass, which amounts to just 17.5 square miles, connects to the Florida mainland where State Road 3 meets U.S. 1 in Volusia County.

Merritt Island is probably best known for its stunning, 140,000-acre national wildlife refuge on a barrier island that also serves as a buffer for rocket launches at the nearby space center. The peninsula itself is home to more than 350 bird species, as well as critters including alligators, bald eagles, bobcats, feral pigs and the stealthy and mysterious official state animal, the Florida panther.

But let's talk crabs, those bottom-dwelling omnivores with sharp front pincers ever at the ready that live throughout the world's tropical and semitropical regions.

The most basic way to catch a crab is by crab lining, using a string, a chicken neck for bait and a small fishing net with a long handle, known as a dip net. It works a lot like fishing: you set the line in the water, then sit and wait for the tug. More serious crabbers use traps, which are large cages fashioned from wire. Bait the trap, wait a day or two and come back for supper—as long as you remember where you set it.

The two most common marine crabs are the blue crab and the Florida stone crab. The blue is mostly fished from the ocean. The stone crab is mostly bought at Joe's Stone Crab restaurant on Miami Beach, the number 1 buyer of the claws and a Florida landmark for more than a century.

"A *Gallo* in Miami?": Fauna and Flora

If you know what you're doing, crabbing is kid stuff. *Ned Horton, freeimages.com.*

Diamond-Storm Hosch's family does its own crabbing. Here is what the young woman, a former student of mine at Florida Atlantic University, will always remember as her first time.

Diamond-Storm Hosch was about seven years old. She's tiny even in her twenties, about five feet even. She was much smaller then—smaller even by the standards of second grade. Her extended family had gathered at her grandmother's house in Sanford, about half an hour northeast of Orlando. Most of them were larger than she. Much larger. Even the children.

The uncles, aunts, cousins and Diamond-Storm's mom sat around the bonfire outside her grandmother's house that first night together, and the conversation turned to crabbing.

"Oh, it's the best!" her mom piped up. "We've got to do that again!"

"Sure," said her grandmother, "but we have to figure out what to do with the little ones." She looked at another daughter. "How would you feel about keeping an eye on them while we're gone?"

Before the woman had time to open her mouth, Diamond-Storm piped up.

"What do you mean, the little ones? Why can't we go with you? It sounds like so much fun, and you never let us have any fun!"

Clearly, she had touched a chord, because several of the other children joined in a chorus of, "We wanna go! We wanna go! Please, please, please! We'll be so good!"

They couldn't be silenced until at last the adults agreed that the next time they went crabbing, the kids would be allowed to come along.

The big day came at last, and the family packed up to go to the beach. When her uncle brought out his big truck, Ruby, and another one brought the boat, the children could barely contain their excitement. The family drove about an hour in several cars, the youngsters all the while jumping up and down in their seats and bragging about how many crabs they planned to catch.

The children were ready to go to work as soon as they reached their destination, but they soon discovered that they were responsible for helping to unpack. For safety, the adults went on the dockside, and the little ones stayed by the road.

True to form and reputation, Diamond-Storm didn't do what she was told. She snuck over to watch what the adults were up to. Several of them were handling not only standard fishing rods, but also cane poles, with the fishing line fitted on one end. Then they took out their crabbing nets, huge drawstring nets made of fine fishing line. The boat was launched, and while her cousins were playing around on the beach, Diamond-Storm watched the grownups execute the tricky maneuver of casting the nets. All the adults were needed on deck to ensure that the lines and ropes didn't tangle. Then she watched them set down each net a good distance from the other, and an uncle went out on a dinghy to arrange the red and white fishing bobbers so they'd remember where they'd put them.

It wasn't till she returned to shore that her mom noticed Diamond-Storm on the bridge.

"Hey!" she scolded. "What are you doing there? Why aren't you with the other kids?"

The little girl shook her head. "Are we gonna start learning how to crab now?"

Her mother smiled. "Okay, fine."

She motioned to an older cousin nearby to assemble all the children. When they were standing in a circle in the sand, she reached for a big Walmart bag. From it, she drew little nets and distributed them out to each child.

But Diamond-Storm was not to be appeased.

"What's this?" she asked, frowning. "I want a net like everybody else."

"Don't you see?" the cousin muttered. "We've all got the same thing."

"I mean I want a net like the grownups have!"

Her mother put her hands on her hips. "You wanted to learn how to crab; go crab. You're not big enough to handle one of those nets! Now go, all of you!"

The child soon got the hang of using the dip net, and she set off to do some crabbing. But it wasn't fun at all. After an hour, she still hadn't found any crabs. Bored nearly to tears and feeling ornery, she made her way back to the other children. The adults, meanwhile, were preparing to return to the boat and pull up their much larger nets.

Diamond-Storm was unsure what to do next, when she spotted a forgotten crab net on a nearby barge. Maybe it was an extra; she had no idea why they'd left it there. But for her, it was a lucky mistake.

Crabs are bottom-dwelling omnivores. *John Boyer, freeimages.com.*

"Now I'll show them," she said aloud. "I'll show them I can crab like the big kids."

The net was so heavy and unwieldy that it took her a few minutes to gather it into her short, skinny arms. It was so long that she kept falling over it. At last, she pulled herself to her feet and got a good grip on the line. But when she tossed it as she'd seen her elders do, she wound up tossing herself, too. Now both she and the net were in the water. The more she struggled to untangle herself, the more tangled she got.

She was not a child to call for help, but she wasn't happy. At last, an older cousin spotted her and jumped into the water to save her. It didn't take long before he scooped her up to safety.

Before she could say a word of thanks, she felt a pinch on her bottom. She looked down, and to her joy, she spotted the culprit. A crab, dangling from her swimsuit! She was so excited that she didn't even feel the pain. A few minutes later, when she was scolded for not following instructions, she didn't mind. Later still, when she took a good look at the red mark left by the pincers, she still didn't mind. She had caught her first crab. And for that, she was allowed to clean it and eat it.

It wasn't a great day for the crab, but Diamond-Storm Hosch was delighted.

30
HANGING WITH THE GATORS

I must admit, I saw the Eisenhower-era image of teenaged Ramona Rung straddling an alligator before talking to her about it—and I fell in love with that photo. Then, after hearing the story, I read up on alligator farms. Somehow, I always thought of them as kind of like petting zoos. Silly me. In fact, these really are serious businesses that breed and raise members of the eight-million-year-old species to eat, carry, sit on or wear.

Internationally, the two-hundred-year-old alligator farming industry is big business. In this country, it extends roughly from Central Texas to North Carolina. In Florida, where the gator is the state's official reptile, there are also more than 1 million of the critters in the wild. That may sound like a lot, but an estimated 10 million were killed by hunters in the South alone between the Civil War and 1962, the year Florida led the nation in protecting the then seriously diminished species. At that point, the population had dwindled to an estimated 100,000, but it is healthy enough today to warrant an alligator hunting season. While Louisiana now produces more alligator products than Florida, the urban legend of our tourists' taking back baby alligators, then flushing them down toilets to the sewers of Manhattan when they're no longer cute, still survives.

Speaking of history, the St. Augustine Alligator Farm Zoological Park dates back to 1893, making it one of the oldest surviving attractions in the state, although it wasn't located at its present address until the 1920s. Now, the venue also boasts crocodiles, Komodo dragons, exotic birds and more.

"A *Gallo* in Miami?": Fauna and Flora

Ramona Rung straddles a new friend near Saint Augustine, circa 1950. *Courtesy of Ramona Rung.*

Ramona is a retired teacher. These days, she entertains children with face-painting and storytelling—which is her first love. That's important to the story. I have known her for years in the local storytelling community, and I called her for her account after seeing the photo on Facebook—which I don't believe was around when she was a girl.

THE YEAR WAS 1950, and the place was Winona, Minnesota. As the first of eight children, the youngest of which was just a toddler, thirteen-year-old Ramona had a lot of obligations at home, what with helping her mother with the cleaning, the grocery shopping and most of all the childcare. It was only at her Catholic school that she felt she could really shine. There she had a boyfriend—meaning they smiled at each other and shared pens and pencils—and she was president of her class. At school, she could imagine herself, one day, being the star she always knew she would be.

Then her father, a construction worker, came home with news.

"Kids," he said one evening at the dinner able, looking at each one of them in turn, even the two-year-old. "I have a big surprise for you."

The chorus of voices spoke up at once.

"A pony?"

"A swimming pool?"

"A baby brother?" At this Ramona's mother shivered and crossed herself.

"No, kids, Dad's got a new job. We're moving to Florida!"

At first, no one said a word. Some of them, admittedly, were too young to know exactly what he was talking about. For Ramona, however, this was just about the worst thing he could say. But as the eldest, she had learned to hold her tongue. It would be hard enough to keep the little ones in line, she knew, without making a scene herself.

"What's a Florida?" one of her little sisters asked.

"Florida," her father replied, "is a big, beautiful, wide open state in the south of this country. It's going to be much warmer than here. We'll be able to go to the beach almost year-round. Imagine that!"

Silence. He looked helplessly at his wife.

"And you know what's *really* great about Florida?" she chimed in, smiling broadly. "You know your cousin's pretty little dark-skinned friend?" They all nodded. "Well, there are plenty of people like that in Florida. You'll love it!"

The thought of meeting exotic people was tantalizing, to be sure. But mainly, Ramona thought of her boyfriend. He was the best-looking guy in the school, and he had chosen *her*! And she had big plans for her role as president, besides. Why would she want to start all over? And more to the point, how could she?

Ramona's dad had been hired as the first superintendent of the Mathews Bridge, a cantilever bridge over the St. Johns River connecting downtown Jacksonville to a neighborhood called Arlington, where they would live. It was a big step up, but that didn't occur to the teen. She just kept telling herself, *I've always wanted to travel. Florida is going to be wonderful. Gotta remember that. It's going to be wonderful.* The family had just recently moved into a comfortable five-bedroom home with a special room in the garage just for bicycles and tools and a beautiful garden. Dad had worked so hard on that garage. But, she was sure, things would be even better in the new house.

"A *Gallo* in Miami?": Fauna and Flora

They needed two cars to make the trip to Florida, and Ramona's mother didn't know how to drive. So the first orders of business were for her to take driving lessons and for him to find a second car. Not six weeks later, they spent more than twenty-four hours driving to Jacksonville, sleeping in cheap motels along the way. It was an adventure, to be sure.

When they arrived at the new house on New Year's Day, 1951, Ramona stood at the front door, rooted to the spot. She couldn't believe her eyes. The place was tiny, a fraction of the size of the place they'd just left. Instead of the lush grass out front, there were pebbles. But it wasn't until she stepped inside that her heart really sank. Where before they had had five bedrooms, now there were just two. In her distress, she walked into the kitchen to get a drink of water.

"Don't—don't drink the water, honey!" her father called out. But it was too late. When she turned on the tap, the foul odor of sulphur permeated the room.

Her father looked at her mother. "Don't worry," he said. "I'll bring water from work."

It got worse. It turned out that it was a distance of more than six miles from Arlington to Jacksonville, where the Catholic school was located. That was too far for the children to make it back and forth on their own. Instead, they enrolled at the local public school, and each Saturday, they attended catechism class.

Ramona was lonely at school, and at home, sharing a room with her three sisters instead of just one like before, quickly began to grate on her nerves. At least on Saturdays, she could shine. Having come from a Catholic school, she knew her lessons far better than her peers. She was the only one who stood up to answer questions, though. Apparently, things were a lot more formal back in Minnesota.

And then one day, not long after the family had settled in, two aunts wrote to say they wanted to bring their children down for a visit.

"They'd like to meet us somewhere fun," Ramona's mother announced, putting down the letter. She turned to her husband. "What do you think?"

"Let me do some research."

They decided on St. Augustine, an easy day trip from Arlington.

"We can also see the Seaquarium on the way back," her father told them.

Her oldest brother piped up. "With the dolphins? They said at school they have dolphins there."

The big day came, and the cousins reunited in Arlington. One of the aunts took one sniff of the sulphur water in the kitchen and turned around for home. But the rest of them took off for St. Augustine. They all loved the quaint streets and the many attractions. And the Seaquarium was everything they'd hoped it would be.

And then they came to the alligator farm. Ramona had never thought much about alligators. They were creepy-looking things with big teeth, to be sure. But she didn't know they were dangerous. Not until her father paid for her, as the eldest, to get inside the pen up close and personal with one of them, that is. When the employee offered to let someone sit on the animal's tail, everyone was too squeamish and fearful to do so. Even the grown men.

"How about you, little lady?"

He was looking at her! Someone in Florida was noticing her!

She nodded, sort of tucked in her chin and took a step forward from the crowd.

"Now, don't be scared, missy!" he murmured. "This one, he's real tame. Ain't nothin' gonna happen to you."

But Ramona hardly noticed what he was saying. She was simply honored to have been chosen. After all, she had always wanted to have people look at her, and here was her big chance. Without another thought, she approached the giant reptile, leaned down and squatted onto the tail. The employee snapped a picture. To the teenager's immense delight, the crowd clapped.

"You okay?" the man asked tentatively. "Had enough?"

At first, she pretended not to hear him. She was so comfortable on the hard, scaly body, she could have sat there all day. But after another minute or two, she stood up and returned to her father.

"You did good, honey," he told her. "You did real good."

"I think I'm going to like it here," she said.

Her father thought she meant Florida. But in fact, she was referring to the limelight.

31
A TURTLE LOVE STORY

Loggerhead. Leatherback. Kemp's Ridley. Hawksbill. Green. These are the five species of sea turtle that populate Florida. And after well over 100 million years on this planet of ours, they're in serious trouble. Florida turtles are threatened not only by human development in their natural habitats but also by what comes with it: pollution, fishing nets, boaters, lights and more.

While the loggerhead is the state's most common turtle, it is the fatty green turtle that early settlers valued most for food. Green turtles, the subject of this story, grow to about 350 pounds. According to the Florida Fish and Wildlife Conservation Commission, 140 years ago, as many as 15,000 green turtles were shipped from Florida and the Caribbean to England each year. In the nineteenth century, that was considered big business.

During the heat of the day, green turtles generally prefer to keep comfortable in sea grass and mate in the shallows. Each evening, it's back to bed on coral reefs, rock ledges and oyster bars. Then from the beginning of March to the end of October, up to one thousand green turtles nest on Florida's beaches. That's when the turtle rangers leap into action like superheroes to save the day—or at least the turtles.

I met Janixx Parisi at the monthly storytelling slam I run in Boca Raton. I had already heard her read her written work and knew that she was a talented writer. But after hearing her tell this story at her first slam performance, I rushed up to hand her my business card. She just had to share her turtle tale for posterity, I said. The biggest challenge in my retelling

Green turtles can grow to about 350 pounds. *Austin Lutz, freeimages.com.*

it here is to capture the emotion in her voice when she talked about finding those poor little hatchlings at the top of the escarpment. Oh, and in case this is a new vocabulary word, an *escarpment* is a long, deep slope.

JANIXX PARISI WAS ALREADY an animal lover when she lived up north in suburban Philadelphia and Washington, D.C. She happily shared her life with cats and dogs and children, and she treated them all with loving care.

Then in 1990, she moved to South Florida. As the owner of an international company that sold parts for commercial aviation, she kept herself busy in a high-powered industry. She didn't have much time for anything else, although as the president of her local chamber of commerce, she gave strong support to the horse show in Wellington.

By 2016, Janixx found herself middle-aged and between relationships. Having met a man she found interesting, she suggested that for their first date, they tour the popular Gumbo Limbo Nature Center in Boca Raton. Mindful that her date wasn't a beach person, she thought they could still get a little fresh air wandering around some of the center's outdoor exhibits, including the garden, boardwalk trail and huge aquariums. The place was pretty crowded with families and tourists, but the two were eventually able to move up close to each glassed-in ecosystem and take a good look.

From the moment she clapped her eyes on the turtle tank, Janixx was in love.

"Look at those big, beautiful guys!" she cried. "And the babies! Absolutely adorable!"

Realizing how she must sound to a stranger, she turned to her date. "You probably think I'm a really gushy person. I'm not, not at all. I've just never seen anything like this before! I *love* these turtles!"

"No problem," he said. "*I* love that you're excited."

When it was time for the two to leave, Janixx felt an unfamiliar tug at her heart. "Can you wait here a minute?" she asked. "I just want to find out something."

"Sure."

"Be right back. I promise."

She strode over to one of the blue-shirted volunteers. "Excuse me," she said. "I'd like to know where I can get an application to work here? Is there someone I can speak to?"

"The manager's right over there," the young man replied, with a wave of his hand. "But I can tell you, there aren't any jobs right now."

"Thanks, I'll check."

She did, and there weren't. But the woman gave her a phone number for the person in nearby Highland Beach who had a permit run, the Florida Wildlife Commission license to coordinate the sea turtle program there.

"You could be a turtle ranger," the manager explained. "You would be on the beach protecting the little guys during nesting season. I don't know if they need more people, but you can try it."

Janixx thanked her and returned to her companion. "Okay," she said. "We can go now."

All through dinner, she thought about those turtles. She liked her date a lot, but she couldn't always keep her mind on what he was saying. After leaving the restaurant, they said their goodnights. And as soon as she walked into the house, she dialed the turtle woman's number. She let the phone ring, ten, twenty times, because, well, you never know.

Janixx called that number every day for weeks. Sometimes, she was able to leave a message. Other times not. Finally, one rainy afternoon, the woman picked up the phone, and Janixx thought she would faint.

"Hello?"

"Hi! I'm Janixx Parisi. I've been calling you…"

"You sure have. I've been in and out of town, and frankly, I don't need any more rangers. But you're persistent, and I like that about you. We need that attitude in this kind of job. Come meet us at the beach tomorrow at sunrise." She gave her some further instructions and hung up, likely not fully realizing how much she had just changed someone's life.

Janixx took to the work right away. Training was intense in both the classroom and on the job. She was fascinated to learn that some of the educators, who were more experienced turtlers, had done this work for sixteen years, some even more. She enjoyed arriving at the beach with the other rangers before sunrise to identify the tracks of the species, determine if they had nested and where, stake the nest and then return once the babies had hatched to dig the nest and take inventory. Sometimes they found live turtles, which they released into the ocean. Sometimes they moved eggs out of harm's way.

Every day there was something new to learn, and Janixx felt grateful for the gift she had given herself the day she signed up. Then in 2018, on the last morning of turtle season, she was walking the beach as usual, mostly picking up plastic and other trash. She had taken to making shell jewelry—every shell she used represented ten pieces of plastic she'd retrieved—and was pocketing some of the prettier little pieces that caught her eye.

There had been a big storm, and while all the baby turtles had hatched, some had been washed out to sea. That was the way it usually happened, she knew. Then she stopped. On her left, atop the six-foot escarpment on the west side of the beach, was a small, dark circle. That meant a nest of baby turtles. It's not easy to climb straight up six feet, but she herringboned her way. What she saw as she approached the top made her queasy. It was the three-toed footprints of raccoons. And raccoons, she knew, eat turtles.

Sure enough, as she drew closer, she saw dozens of hatchlings. Not one of them was moving. Devastated, Janixx fell to her knees. What a terrible legacy, she thought, on the last day of the season. All these turtles, dead. Sure, she told herself, raccoons have to eat, too. But raccoons aren't endangered.

That's when she realized that the baby turtles were still intact. It hadn't been raccoons after all. They would have ripped them apart from head to toe. It had to have been the sun that got to them. If only they had hatched at night like they were supposed to! She wondered if someone had shone a bright light somewhere nearby. Lights at night confuse the turtles into hatching at the wrong time, which is why coastal towns have ordinances against them too close to the beach.

Whatever the cause of death, she knew what she had to do. It was a ritual she had undertaken since she'd started as a ranger. She picked up the baby closest to her, rose to her feet and set off toward the surf.

"You're going back to where you belong," she murmured, fighting back tears as she petted the tiny head. "You did such a good job breaking out of that shell. I'm really proud of you. I'm just sorry you didn't make it. I'm sorry I didn't get here in time."

Janixx knew it wasn't her fault. She knew a turtle's odds of making it were slim, with only one out of a thousand hatchlings actually surviving to maturity. Then she thought of the babies' mother, born on this same beach thirty or so years before. And despite her knowledge and experience, her eyes filled with tears. She came here to Highland Beach every day, twice a day! How hadn't she spotted this nest before? Why hadn't someone else? Why was nature so cruel?

She had almost reached the water's edge when all at once she felt some movement in her hands. She looked down and gasped. The turtle was weakly turning its head and fluttering its flippers. It was alive.

First, she leaned down and blew a kiss to the little head. Then she sprinted back for her bucket. The adrenaline helped her climb back up the escarpment in no time. She gently set down the baby turtle in her bucket and turned to the others. One by one she picked up each unmoving turtle. And one by one they came to life in her hands. By the time the sun rose, she had collected fifty-four live baby turtles.

Janixx ran to her car and sped over to Gumbo Limbo. She pounded on the door until a bleary-eyed man came to open it and then handed him the bucket with a brief explanation. At last, she made her way home, puzzling over what had happened. Maybe she had scared off the raccoons, and the babies were in shock. Maybe they had suffered a bit of sunstroke. In any case, if someone hadn't come along, she knew, either the sun would have fried them or the birds would have picked them off. It happened all the time.

Two days later, she called Gumbo Limbo. When she heard that an employee had taken the fully recovered baby turtles to the sea, she poured herself a glass of wine to celebrate. She drank it alone. Her relationship with her Gumbo Limbo date had ended some time earlier, although they were still friends. But she knew she would care for those turtles forever. She had fallen in love on the first date.

32

BEATING THE BLUES

On February 14, 2019, the headline of an online news story from Newark, New Jersey public radio WBGO read, "After 16 Months of Dead Fish, Manatees and Dolphins, Florida's Red Tide Ebbs." Underneath was a line of dead fish lying along an otherwise pristine shoreline.

The toxic bloom of red tide that periodically terrorizes the Gulf Coast is caused by the higher than normal proliferation of an alga called *Karenia brevis*, brought about by poor water quality and pollution and exacerbated by higher than normal water temperatures. On the state's east coast, another HAB (harmful algae bloom), the less well-known blue-green algae, recently caused the water in the St. Lucie River estuary to be deemed ten times more toxic than acceptable. Suspected health conditions that stem from ingesting the microcystin it contains range from nausea to Alzheimer's disease.

Becky Harris lives on the St. Lucie River. I reached her by phone after her daughter Samantha, a former student of mine, told me her mother had an only-in-Florida story I wouldn't soon forget. Neither will you.

When Becky arranged to meet her daughter for lunch at a restaurant in Palm Beach, she was expecting salad, not a five-pound mini Pomeranian.

"What is this?" she said, reaching instinctively for the pooch. The two cats and dog that lived with her couldn't begin to satisfy her love for animals.

"This is Pandora," Samantha said.

"Wow! You just got her, huh?"

"A *Gallo* in Miami?": Fauna and Flora

Dealing with the effects of toxic algae washed ashore is no day at the beach. *Chris Petescia, freeimages.com.*

The nineteen-year-old picked up her fork and twirled it around her fingers before answering.

"Actually," she said, not quite meeting her mother's eyes, "I've had her for four months."

"What?" Becky was a little shocked. After all, they spoke on the phone all the time, and they only lived an hour apart. "Four months! Why didn't you say anything?"

"Well, I guess I didn't think you'd approve. I couldn't keep her in the dorm, so I gave her to my friend. Turns out he's allergic." She sighed. "Guess we'll have to get rid of her."

"You'll do no such thing!" Becky found herself holding the dog a little tighter without meaning to. "We'll—I'll keep her for a while, see what your dad says. Let's not do anything hasty."

So it was that Pandora accompanied Becky home, and less than a week later, she had become part of the family. Becky immediately noticed that her daughter hadn't done much of a training job on her pet. She taught her to ask to go out when she needed to, as well as a few rudimentary commands. Before long, the pair had earned dog therapy certification and began visiting nursing homes to entertain the residents or schools to teach the children about basic pet care. Becky never tired of seeing the smiles light up people's faces when they met Pandora. More than once, the sight brought tears to her eyes.

One day, she took both of her dogs to the beach behind the house as usual. Their routine was to run a little, do their business, sniff around. After a while, Pandora seemed to be fussing with something at the shoreline, and Becky ran over to see. It was a dead fish.

"Drop it!" she yelled. "Drop it, Pandora!"

But the little dog ran behind a stand of sea grapes and finished off her treat before Becky could reach her.

That evening, the Harrises held a small dinner party. All of the sudden, Pandora, who had been lying quietly on the floor, vomited. Becky had already noticed that she was a little logy and limp. Thinking the dog might be dehydrated from the run on the beach, she filled up her water bowl and took it over to her. To Becky's shock, the dog's tiny neck was too weak to raise her head, which fell into the water.

Making apologies to her guests, she raced the dog to an all-night vet, thinking she would need an IV and that she could take her home that night. Instead, the doctor emerged from the back and asked her a few questions. Had Pandora been exposed to rat poison? What about sago palms or poisonous mushrooms? Sugarless gum? Raccoon urine or feces?

"No," she said. "Although I did see her eat a dead fish on the beach today."

"She'll need to stay overnight," the doctor said.

"What for? What's the matter?"

"I can't say." The woman pursed her lips. "We drew blood, but it's still not clotting. That's not a good sign. We've got her on an IV, and we're giving her antibiotics. All we can do at this stage is start treating her for leptospirosis and see what happens."

Becky hadn't fully absorbed all this when the doctor continued, "Preliminary results from the blood test show that her liver is failing. So we've got her on liver support drugs as well. We'll know more tomorrow."

How she drove home, Becky wasn't sure. She just kept thinking about that fish. It hadn't looked strange, but what was it doing, lying dead on the beach like that?

The next morning, the veterinarian called again with more bad news. Pandora's platelets were low; she was experiencing acute liver failure.

"We're sending her over to the specialist next door," she continued. "We've worked out a five-day treatment plan. And I have to tell you, it isn't going to be cheap."

"A *Gallo* in Miami?": Fauna and Flora

This was all moving very fast for Becky.

"Wait a minute," she said. "Let's take one day at a time. What does she need first?"

"We're doing a plasma transfusion," the veterinarian said. "And continuous IV fluid, antibiotics and liver support meds."

She couldn't quite believe she was forming the words: "Is she dying?"

"I've got to tell you, Mrs. Harris, I've never seen it this bad before. I've seen the problem, though. This is the seventh dog I've treated lately with these symptoms. I can't promise you anything. I'm really sorry. But we'll do our best."

Becky called Samantha as soon as she got into the car.

"You've got to come up, honey. Pandora is really sick. We don't know if she's going to make it." There was a pause on the other end of the line. "Sam, do you hear me?"

"I'll be there as fast as I can, Mom."

Samantha stayed at the house a couple of days, driving back and forth to classes in Boca Raton. At one point, Becky brought her other dog's collar to the animal hospital so Pandora could smell her and be reminded of home.

By the second day, the vet was so pessimistic that Becky called an in-home pet euthanasia service.

"Shall we schedule an appointment for tomorrow?" the pleasant voice said.

Becky hesitated. Something told her to wait.

"I'll get back to you," she said.

And then, miraculously, over the next four or five days in the ER, Pandora steadily improved. She even started eating again. Meanwhile, a chihuahua mix that lived on the river came in with the exact same symptoms.

One night, Becky was on Facebook when a friend sent her a post from another veterinarian, saying that his colleagues in the area had seen three cases of liver failure.

"Three other cases?" she said out loud. She contacted the vet, and from there she contacted the owner. The dog, a golden retriever named Costa, also lived on the river.

When Pandora was released from the hospital at last, Becky returned to talk to her vet.

"This has got to be the algae," she said. "It's everywhere. I think we should go public with this. To save other dogs."

The woman shook her head. "I sympathize, Mrs. Harris, I really do," she said. But I'm a scientist. I can't prove it's the algae. I don't want to get people worked up about this without proof."

So instead, Becky called Ashley, Costa's owner.

"Let's go to the media together," she said. "We'll give the information to that Channel 12 reporter Erin McPherson, and the one at Channel 25, and we'll contact the paper, too."

So it was that on Labor Day, three reporters arrived at the house to conduct interviews. Unfortunately, four more dogs had been affected, and a black poodle had died. One of the dogs had been running along the St. Lucie Canal, ate some grass and became very sick. His owner had to pick him up and carry him home.

Eventually, every dog affected was confirmed to have had microcystins in its vomit and urine. Their owners took the obvious next step: they met with their congressman. To their dismay, his marching orders were to keep this from the media.

"But this is a human and health safety problem," Becky protested. "These are the canaries in the coal mine! We're next!"

Becky, who had been working as a bookkeeper for her family's business and other clients, began attending South Florida Water Management meetings, and meeting with the lieutenant colonel of the Army Corps of Engineers. Then her husband suggested she do something bigger. So she created toxicdischarges.com.

Soon it got even bigger. She heard that Erin Brockovich, the famous environmental activist played in the movies by Julia Roberts, was coming to nearby Satellite Beach. Becky invited her to Stuart, where she held a press conference with that same congressman. Their work eventually led to the Stop the Harmful Discharges Act, which encourages the Corps to help prevent the scourge of blue-green algae by keeping the lake at lower levels prior to the wet season.

And so environmental activism became pretty much a full-time job for Becky Harris. She met with fellow dog owners. She gained an understanding of lake discharges, polluters and protected species like the sea sparrow. It was an uphill climb to make changes. But she wouldn't have had it any other way.

33

THE NATURE OF NATURE

Tiger Creek Preserve is owned and managed by the Nature Conservancy, the charitable environmental organization that has protected land and rivers throughout the world since 1951. Located in central Florida, the preserve is set on the eastern edge of the Lake Wales Ridge, a former island that bears the distinction of being the highest landmass on the peninsula. According to the organization, the concentration of threatened and endangered plants and animals in the preserve is among the nation's highest, with some so rare that they can be found nowhere else on the planet.

I met Steve Morrison when I stopped in with a mutual friend on my way to perform in Polk County. For more than three decades, he and his father, Ken, before him have played a critical role in the five-thousand-acre preserve. Steve lives in a rustic setting that is nothing less than you would expect from a land manager for the Nature Conservancy: a cozy, two-floor cabin, complete with outhouse out back, a creek within spitting distance and acres of private wilderness all around.

This story's surprising happy ending—and I hope you agree we can call it that—is the reason I chose to place it last in the book. Let it stand as a note of comfort and hope for this magnificent state at a time of great challenges and greater change.

STEVE MORRISON MAY HAVE been born in a suburb of New York City, but he has had a lifelong interest in the natural world, particularly after moving to Florida's Polk County as a small boy. He came by it naturally. His dad had

Only in Florida

Marshland has returned to the Tiger Creek Preserve. David Fowler.

been the editor of *Audubon* magazine, and he went on to become a longtime director of Bok Tower Gardens, a central Florida landmark. His mother in turn was an environmental educator, the kind who rehabilitated injured wild animals and took them into local schools.

It was a good thing Steve shared his parents' ethos. Otherwise, the presence of ailing egrets in the bathtub and foxes in the bedroom might have fazed him. Instead, he loved sharing his home with wild and beautiful creatures.

In 1987, the Nature Conservancy hired Steve as a land manager for one of its Florida crown jewels: the Tiger Creek Preserve, which his father and mother had helped found. Steve took the job seriously. Managing the land entails ensuring that nature gets to function normally, meaning a good deal of the job consists of undoing what harm humans have done. One of his most important tasks was to execute controlled burns—fires that would have occurred naturally to clear out dead brush and make way for new growth, except that residential development and the firefighting it requires prevented their doing so. He also planted trees, cleared nonnative species and erected barriers to prevent further destruction of the land.

Over the years, Steve and his team of employees and volunteers put in long days getting to know the area so well that they could observe the smallest changes in habitats. In 2004, after a series of three hurricanes descended on the area, there was no doubt that the land had been bruised. But nature is nature, and they knew it was resilient.

"A *Gallo* in Miami?": Fauna and Flora

It wasn't until a couple of years later that Steve and his team noticed something strange. They didn't catch it all at once, but little by little over the course of a few weeks, they noticed that the thousand or so acres that had been swamp forest had changed. The red maple, red and loblolly bay and other trees that had been there when he first came to the preserve had died and fallen into the swamp, creating a kind of dam that backed up the water even more than the storms had. This created a domino effect in which the water kept rising even higher, causing more and more trees to die.

Steve was horrified. "I don't understand," he told a colleague one day at lunch. "It seems like this broad-leafed swamp forest is turning into an open marsh."

"You're right. There's too much water. It's been high for over a year. Instead of trees, we've got aquatic vegetation. Swamp willow, button bush, sawgrass."

"I've never seen anything like it. But what could be causing it?"

"The storms, maybe? Three storms so close together, that could be a sign of climate change."

"Could be." He shrugged. "The hurricanes did a lot of damage, knocking off the tops of trees and such. But this devastating stuff, this tree death, it didn't start until more recently."

"Or it could be chemicals. Who knows? The question is, how are we going to fix this?"

It wasn't that Steve couldn't deal with change. He was, after all, a prescribed burner. He knew about plants being killed by fire. But by flooding? He grew more and more disturbed. What on earth was going on? And what would it take to make it right?

Steve and his team puzzled over the mystery for quite some time. Then one day in 2006, he was looking at some aerial photographs taken of the area in 1921. With an eye toward buying the land, Edward Bok had hired a New York company to shoot photos, and Frederick Law Olmsted of New York's Central Park fame, to make maps.

As land manager, Steve had gotten hold of the photos and maps years before. But this time, he examined them more closely. And what he found shocked him up off his seat.

Marsh! The 1921 aerial photos showed marshlands where Steve had known only forested swamp. And Olmsted's map even had "sawgrass" written over the area Steve has known only as swamp. He strode over to his colleague's office, documents in hand.

"It's okay!" he said, waving the photo. "It's all okay!"

"What are you talking about, Steve?"

"The land. The swamp forest. It shows right here that it used to be marsh. This isn't global warming at all! It's a cycle!"

"If what you're saying is true…."

"I'm sure it's true! Just look at the evidence."

The man spent many minutes poring over the photograph and map. When he looked up at Steve, his grin was huge.

"So that explains it," he said. "This is all perfectly normal."

"The cycle of life," Steve replied, matching the man's smile with his own. "It's not development. It's not toxic waste. It's not even climate change. It's just plain old nature, doing its thing—on a time scale so long, you have to be here a long time to experience it.

"This time," he repeated, because it felt so good to say, "it's just nature, doing its thing."

SELECTED BIBLIOGRAPHY

Allen, Greg. "After 16 Months of Dead Fish, Manatees and Dolphins, Florida's Red Tide Ebbs." WBGO. February 14, 2019. www.wwno.org.

Authentic Florida. authenticflorida.com.

Daily Commercial. dailycommercial.com

Edgerley, Len. "Portrait of a Sponge Diver." medium.com.

Flatsmasters. flatsmasters.com.

Florida Fish and Wildlife Conservation Commission. myfwc.com.

@Floridaman, Twitter.

Florida State Parks. floridastateparks.org.

Florida State University Emergency Management. emergency.fsu.edu/resources/hazards/lightning.

The Founders Golf Club. thefoundersgolfclub.com.

Golf. golf.com

Haskell, Arlo. *The Jews of Key West: Smugglers, Cigar Markers, and Revolutionaries*. Key West, FL: Sand Paper Press, 2017.

Hill, Logan. "Is It Okay to Laugh at the Florida Man Meme?" *Washington Post*, July 15, 2019. washingtonpost.com.

Kings Point Golf and Country Club. kingspointdelray.com.

Know Your Meme. "Florida Man." knowyourmeme.com.

Marr, Madeleine. "Florida Man 2018. A Look Back at Florida's Most Florida Crime Stories." miamiherald.com.

McGinniss, Joe. *Going to Extremes*. Kenmore, WA: Epicenter Press, 2010.

National Weather Service. weather.gov.

Selected Bibliography

Oliver, Kitty. *Multicolored Memories of a Black Southern Girl*. Lexington: University Press of Kentucky, 2001.
Orlando Weekly. "These Vintage Photos Show Disney World's Evolution from Florida Project to 'the Most Magical Place on Earth.'" photos.orlandoweekly.com.
Palm Beach Post. palmbeachpost.com.
Shaw, George Bernard. *Misalliance*. Project Gutenberg. www.gutenberg.org.
South Florida Sun Sentinel. sunsentinel.com.
Tampa Bay Times. tampabay.com.
Tanya the Mango Lady Blog. tanyathemangoladyblog.org.
United States Census Bureau. www.census.gov.
Universal Studios. universalorlando.com.
World Golf Hall of Fame. worldgolfhalloffame.org.

ABOUT THE AUTHOR

Caren Schnur Neile, PhD, MFA, is a performance storyteller who has taught storytelling studies at Florida Atlantic University since 2001. Dr. Neile has appeared and published throughout the country and abroad, including as a university instructor in Warsaw, Poland, and as a Fulbright Senior Specialist in universities in Jerusalem, Israel, and Vienna, Austria. She is the former chair of the National Storytelling Network and a former founding editor of the international academic journal *Storytelling, Self, Society*. Prior to her storytelling career, Caren served with the U.S. Peace Corps in South Korea and worked for the news department at WPIX-TV in New York City.

Dr. Neile co-hosts and produces The Public Storyteller, a weekly segment on South Florida public radio WLRN 91.3 FM. Her numerous publications include an entry in the Oxford University Press *Handbook of American Folklore and Folklife*, the book *Florida Lore* for The History Press and a biweekly column on storytelling for the *Florida Jewish Journal*. She has been featured in *Cosmopolitan* magazine, *The Toastmaster*, *Die Zeit* (Germany) and other media.

Visit us at
www.historypress.com